TIME AND SELF

American Academy of Religion
Studies in Religion
39

Editors
Charley Hardwick
James O. Duke

TIME AND SELF
Phenomenological Explorations

Paul Brockelman

THE CROSSROAD PUBLISHING COMPANY
&
SCHOLARS PRESS

The Crossroad Publishing Company
370 Lexington Avenue
New York, NY 10017

Scholars Press
P.O. Box 1608
Decatur, GA 30031-1608

Library of Congress Cataloging in Publication Data

Brockelman, Paul T.
  Time and self.

  (AAR studies in religion ; 39)
  1. Self (Philosophy). 2. Time. I. Title. II. Series:
Studies in religion (American Academy of Religion) ; 39.
BD450.B6496 1985   126   84–13994
ISBN 0–8245–0703–7 (pbk. : alk. paper)
ISBN 0–89130–779–6 (Scholars Press : hard : alk. paper)
ISBN 0–89130–780–X (Scholars Press : pbk. : alk. paper)

Printed in the United States of America

To Barbara

At bottom, the ordinary is not ordinary, it is extra-ordinary.
Heidegger, *The Origin of the Work of Art*

Contents

PREFACE

This book is in part and in a modest way an essay which sets out to explore and clarify what it means to be a self, especially in relation to time. I say "in part" because one book of course can never hope to complete the analysis of such a topic; and "in a modest way" because there is no claim here to infallible or conclusive truth, or for that matter even comprehensiveness. In other words, there are more issues to get at than are gotten at here, and there is surely a lot more to say about even those issues we do touch.

More specifically, there are four interrelated goals I hope to achieve in this phenomenological exploration: (1) to outline those aspects and structures of our temporal action and experience which might help us better to understand what it means to be a self; (2) to isolate the dimension of life-value or human attitude toward life within that everyday temporal activity and to point out the centrality of such attitudes in the development of personal identity; (3) to show in some detail the theory of temporal and narrative self to which my analysis leads; and (4) to indicate how such a view of time and self might come to grips with certain traditional issues in the philosophy of self.

In many ways, this is a study which finds itself "in between." First of all, it is "in between" in the sense that it is neither a full phenomenology of time nor a complete theory of self, but rather an exploration of the difficult ground between. On the one hand, I deal only with those elements of a philosophy of time which can help us get at what it means to be a self. On the other hand, I focus only on those aspects of self which are temporal in nature, leaving out for example any discussion of the obvious social dimensions of ourselves. Those seeking either a full analysis of time or a complete theory of self will have to look elsewhere, or at least develop them beyond the scope of this book.

This essay is "in between" in another way. The territory I am exploring falls between the traditional fields of philosophy, psychology, literary theory, and religious studies; for we shall be led from a philosophy of time to a view of personal identity with serious implications for our understanding of religious attitude and faith. In the process, I shall develop the transcendental argument that the various realms of narrative discourse through which human beings find life construed with meaning (novels, stories, sacred history, drama, mythology, theology, history) find their existential roots in the temporal and narrative structure of personal identity. Without the narrative condition involved in being a "self," there could be no literature, history, poetry, or religion.[1] It is difficult and dangerous to enter such interdisciplinary territory: one risks communicating with no one at all! Yet, perhaps just because it lies in between and beneath those sovereign kingdoms, I think it is a rich area with significance for each.

In this period of comparative religion, anthropology, and the theory of deconstruction, we are all very aware of an evident relativity of value and attitude from person to person and culture to culture. That certainly includes a relativity concerning what kinds of selves various cultures foster and support as well as a relativity concerning where and to what we should look to discover what personal identity means. Is there an Eastern sense of "self" as opposed to a Western one, for example; a male as opposed to a female; or a young as opposed to an old? And is the very notion of a phenomenology—whether of time or self—culturally biased? These are excellent questions, but not ones which I can hope to resolve within the bounds of this essay. Although I would claim that phenomenology done properly is a necessary preliminary to dealing with such questions, the doing of that phenomenology as such does not directly answer them. In short, a study such as this cannot deal with everything; it is enough if we can simply clear some of the ground.

As both St. Augustine and David Hume so richly demonstrated, reflection on the nature and relationship of time and self is not only notoriously difficult, but actually bursting with perplexities and paradoxes. Augustine in his *Confessions* and Hume in the *Treatise on Human Nature*, for example, reached the startling conclusion that they could in fact conclude nothing at all about self. Along the way, both admit to confusion and even a little bit of anxiety, for it would seem that nothing could be more intimately related to "self" than these two "selves." And if they were reduced to confusion and anxiety by their struggles to understand the nature of self, both were left absolutely mired in perplexity when they were led inevitably to think about the related philosophical issue of time. In the classic words of Augustine:

> For what is time? Who can readily and briefly explain this? Who can even in thought comprehend it, so as to utter a word about it? But what in discourse do we mention more familiarly and knowingly, than time? And, we understand, when we speak of it; we understand also when we hear it spoken of by another. What

---

[1] Paul Ricoeur, whose recent book, *Time and Narrative*, I received only after this monograph was already in galley form, points to just such an argument and extends it into a very rich analysis of the creation of meaning at the level of the narrative text. See Paul Ricoeur, *Time and Narrative*, trans. Kathleen McLaughlin and David Pellauer (Chicago: University of Chicago Press, 1984), vol. 1, esp. pp. 52, 54, 60, 64.

then is time? If no one asks me, I know: if I wish to explain it to one that asketh, I know not.[2]

Why another study of "time" and "self," then? How could anyone run through this particular gauntlet again? It is for three reasons: (1) because the nature of time and self are so perplexing and because philosophical history is strewn with the wreckage of so many failures to deal with it adequately; (2) because it just happens to be important in philosophy, psychology, religious studies, and intellectually in general; and (3) because I think a phenomenological analysis of action and time constitutes a relatively fresh approach to self which can, I hope, lead to something other than paradoxes and nonconclusions.

This is a "phenomenological" study. Since that term is interpreted in widely varying ways, I want to make a brief comment about it in order to forestall misunderstanding. This essay is an "existential" phenomenology rather than a "pure" phenomenology in the line of Husserl, Alfred Schutz, or even Maurice Natanson, however indebted I am to these remarkable thinkers in other respects. What that means is that rather than a transcendental and eidetic analysis of consciousness to itself, we are striving here (in the line of Merleau-Ponty and Ricoeur, for example) phenomenologically to describe and evoke the temporal dimension of our actual bodily experience and activity in the world. It is an attempt to make reflective and give voice to our prereflective and mute experience, or at least those temporal aspects we will find helpful in dealing with issues facing any philosophy of self.[3]

What follows, then, is a sort of intellectual, archaeological investigation. That is, it is an attempt phenomenologically to dig down into, explore, and to sift out some fundamental aspects of our ordinary lives and experience which often remain hidden and unavailable to reflective consciousness, because they are covered over with layers of culture, linguistic, and philosophical sedimentation. More specifically, we want to get at and lay out some significant elements of the personal dimension of our lives by means of a careful phenomenological analysis of action and temporality from the point of view of the human agent. That analysis, I think, will lead to a rather different way to deal with the various problems and issues strewn across the field of self.

The natural *order of interest* for a phenomenological study such as this is to go from the familiar to the less familiar, the ordinary to the

---

[2] Augustine, *The Confessions of St. Augustine*, trans. E. B. Pusey (New York: Dutton, 1966), p. 262.

[3] For more on the distinction between these two kinds of phenomenology and, in particular, the nature of "existential phenomenology," see Paul Brockelman, *Existential Phenomenology and the World of Ordinary Experience: An Introduction* (Lanham, MD: University Press of America, 1980), as well as Chapter Five following.

special, the concrete and everyday to the more abstract structural relations within it. I want to carry the reader from his or her familiar world of practical activity to the more abstract dimension of personal identity and structure of self. Although this is not a specifically "religious book," I think that Karl Rahner, in a recent article entitled "The Future of the Religious Book," has put well the order embodied in this essay.

> It can do no harm if the religious book of the future begins with matters which seem to be in the foreground, for it is these that constitute the realities of life. It must begin, then, with human activities—with work, love, death, and all the well-worn and familiar matters with which human life is filled.[4]

The *philosophical order* of this book happens to parallel that natural *order of interest*. In the first part, "The Problem of Self," we outline what the "problem" is and the traditional issues associated with any philosophy of self. Part Two, "Exploring the Temporal Conditions of Self," sets the stage for our phenomenological approach to self by describing the structure of our temporal actions and our reflective consciousness of it. Part Three, finally, "Self," outlines a view of a personal identity and self based on those temporal conditions, a view which, I hope, permits us to come to grips with the traditional issues in a productive way.

I am grateful for permission to reprint here, in revised form, parts of the following essays: "Action and Time," *Man and World* 10, number 3, 1977; "Myths and Stories: The Depth Dimension of Our Lives," *Philosophy Today* 24, Spring 1980; and "The Awareness of Time," *Research in Phenomenology* xi, 1981.

I am also grateful to the College of Liberal Arts at the University of New Hampshire for granting me sabbatical leave to finish this monograph and for providing the technical resources to prepare the penultimate manuscript version.

I also want to express appreciation to my editor, Professor Charley Hardwick of the American University, for the time he took with the manuscript and for the significant improvements in this essay which his close reading of the text entailed.

Finally, I want to thank both Susan Goodman and Jackie Kraus for the real improvements they effected in the manuscript.

---

[4] Karl Rahner, "The Future of the Religious Book," *The New Review of Books and Religion*, Feb., 1979, p. 6.

PART ONE:
THE PROBLEM OF SELF

Chapter One
WHAT DO WE MEAN BY SELF?

> There are at present no easy answers to the big questions, and it
> will take radical rethinking of the issues before people can be
> expected to reach a consensus about the meaning of the word "I."
> —Douglas Hofstadter and Daniel Dennett, *The Mind's I*

Of all the issues and human concerns which have fascinated and
frustrated philosophers over the years, that of the meaning or nature of
"self" or "personal identity" has been one of the most persistent and
perplexing, in spite of the fact that that is just what each of us happens
to be. While the variety of approaches and perspectives has grown, the
amount of agreement and mutual understanding certainly has not.

The self has been conceived in a wide variety of ways. For example,
it is sometimes thought of as reducible to physical, psychological, or perhaps behavioral terms and conditions. It has been looked at as simply
nonexistent, the result of a grammatical constraint forced upon us by the
structure of our language, in other words, the subject of attribution.[1]
Some see it as a soul inhabiting the body temporarily and some as the
"experiencer" not itself susceptible to experience. So-called "cognitive
scientists" think of "mind" and "self" not as computers but as very complex software programs. And Sartre, of course, thinks it is a "nothing"
which in a middle-class sort of way is trying very hard to be something!
At any rate, whether the self be nothing or everything, always there or
constructed out of discrete moments, an empty and transcendental
ground of all unity or a full but momentary monad which constructs its
shadow out of its own memory, the variety of perspectives is bewilder-
ingly impressive. When you add to that the remarkable gulfs and abysses
which seem to separate these divergent views, you begin to get a sense of
the dimensions of the issue we face. The issue is very perplexing.

It was Bergson who pointed out that the traditional philosophical
approaches to the problem of self have tended to fall into two extreme and
dialectically opposed metaphysical positions. On the one hand, we have the
"empiricists" who attempt to "reconstruct personality with psychical

---

[1] Strawson calls this the "no-ownership" or "no-subject" theory of self and ascribes it to
views which both Wittgenstein and Schlick held at one or another time in their lives. See
P. F. Strawson, *Individuals* (Garden City, NY: Doubleday, 1963), pp. 89–90.

states,"[2] i.e., a series of temporally separate, empirical egos which can never find their way together into a single unity. On the other hand, we have what Bergson calls the "rationalists," who posit the unity of "self" in a transcendental identity which can never quite account for the fragmentation and diversity of actual empirical egos over time, because it is beyond or behind them.[3] Seemingly endlessly swinging back and forth between these polar opposites, our metaphysical tradition has viewed the self as either invented at each moment by its own present memory or as a pristine and untouched entity above and beyond the humdrum process of change through time.

There is a certain element of humor about all this, as when Hume, one of those very "selves" he is trying to understand, shockingly enough is not able to find himself. He becomes lost in a tangled conceptual "labyrinth,"[4] he tells us, because he can never quite "catch" his actual self in a simple and constant impression *over* time. Instead, he only "stumbles on some particular perception or other, of heat or cold, light or shade, love or hatred, pain or pleasure." As he says, "I never can catch *myself.*"[5]

Bertrand Russell, not to be outdone in this remarkable affair, commits a sort of metaphysical suicide right before our eyes. In *The Analysis of Mind*, he decides that his person or self is not really an essential ingredient in his own thinking, but is "rather constituted by relations of thoughts to each other," just as Hume had earlier contended. It would be far better in our grammatical usages not to say "I think," but "it thinks in me, like it rains here."[6] If not humorous, it is certainly startling and noteworthy to watch a philosopher do away with himself on the printed page, and in favor of a grammatical locution at that!

But lest we be led to think the humor lies only on the one empiricist side of this issue, it is only fair to point out that what Bergson calls "rationalism" (which might be better termed "idealism") has its own brand of humor with respect to the self; witness the attitude of the contemporary American philosopher, William Earle, for example. Here we have an actual person or self in and through time positing an "absolute," "timeless," and "eternal" transcendental ego which—although in no way empirically verifiable and entirely empty of content, since it is the root condition of all empirical knowledge and ego-content—is *nevertheless*

---

[2] Henri Bergson, *An Introduction to Metaphysics*, trans. T. E. Hulme (New York: G. P. Putnam's Sons, 1912), p. 30.

[3] Bergson, *Introduction*, p. 33.

[4] David Hume, *Treatise on Human Nature*, ed. L. A. Selby-Bigge (Oxford: The Clarendon Press, 1973), Appendix, p. 633.

[5] Hume, *Treatise*, p. 252.

[6] Bertrand Russell, *The Analysis of the Mind* (London: G. Allen and Unwin Ltd., 1921), pp. 17–18.

the basis of the unity which ties together the temporal series of empirical egos into one self, just this William Earle.[7] A strange endeavor this "positing" of an empty and unperceivable substance by a very real self to account *for* itself.

Now if all of this is amusing, it is primarily because we have abstracted it out of its serious philosophical context. Clearly there *are* real questions about what we mean by "self" and/or "personal identity." In fact, that issue has increasingly moved to the center of the philosophical stage. In the words of Amelie Rorty, "the concept of *person* now emerges as dominant in philosophical analysis and in social life,"[8] probably because of our present concern and conflict about ethical value, law and social responsibility. After all, one can never deal adequately with these practical and social questions without anchoring choice and responsibility in a viable notion of agency and self.[9]

What distinguishes the class of entities called "selves" from other classes such as "animals," "machines," or "things?" After all, we do not treat real persons like machines, nor would we treat machines like persons. We would not charge a machine with "murder," for example, or take it to court. We would not demand that it be "responsible" and punish it if it were not. Yet we do just that with ourselves and others. On the

---

[7] See William Earle, *The Autobiographical Consciousness* (Chicago: Quadrangle Books, 1972), pp. 60, 61, 62, 67. We have chosen *not* to include Edmund Husserl and his notion of "Transcendental Ego" in this category for the simple reason that if he is an idealist with respect to the self, he is surely a very different kind than Earle. For Husserl, the Transcendental or Pure Ego is the structure of the field of intentional consciousness reflexively aware of itself. As such, it is "absolute" and "original." So far so good. But unlike Earle, who finds the unity of such transcendental consciousness logically prior to and outside the structure of time into which it "falls," for Husserl the Transcendental Ego is "not ultimate" but has its "primal source in what is ultimately and truly absolute," namely the structure of "internal time." "The *Unity of the immanent time-consciousness. . .* is the all-enveloping unity of *consciousness* that binds consciousness with consciousness." Thus, Husserl does not seem to reduce "self" to a transcendental something behind or beyond the flow of time and which reaches over and through it to bind it into one, as is commonly supposed of him. On the contrary, the unity of the Transcendental Self or Ego is itself constituted out of the binding structure of time. In this respect, we shall follow Husserl's (and Heidegger's and Bergson's) lead in analyzing self in terms of time rather than vice versa. For more on this, see Edmund Husserl, *Ideas*, trans. W. R. Boyce Gibson (New York: Collier Books, 1972), pp. 216, 307; also, for a very interesting discussion of this issue, see Ronald P. Morrison, "Kant, Husserl, and Heidegger on Time and the Unity of Consciousness," *Philosophy and Phenomenological Research* 39 (1978):182ff.

[8] Amelie O. Rorty, "A Literary Postscript," in *The Identities of Persons*, ed. Amelie Rorty (Los Angeles: University of California Press, 1976), p. 320.

[9] Rorty, *Identities*, p. 320. Also, see Alan Gewirth, *Reason and Morality* (Chicago: University of Chicago Press, 1978), sec. 1:13. Prof. Gewirth argues rather cogently that moral judgements ultimately find their justification in "statements or judgements that are necessarily attributable to every agent because they derive from the generic features that constitute the necessary structure of action."

other hand, normally we would not treat a person like a "machine" or a "thing." If for some reason we did, we might expect personal and legal repercussions. Why? What separates these realities into the kinds of entities they are? What *kind* of an entity is a self or person? What characteristics make it what it is, just this class and not another?

Even our ordinary language is pervaded by this distinction between ourselves and other entities. Impersonal pronouns refer to nonpersons, and personal pronouns to persons. "Thus, the problem of explicating the concept of self is the problem of explaining what, for each of us, is the referent to the first-person pronoun."[10]

What follows is a phenomenological exploration of the nature of self within our ordinary experience. We shall get at that by first trying to lay out the temporal structure of action from the point of view of the agent involved. That view of "temporality" as opposed to "objective time," I am claiming, provides a foundation on which we can at least begin to develop a more adequate theory of self than those of our recent philosophical past.

But why "time," you might ask? Why should a phenomenological analysis of time help us get at the nature of "self"? First of all, there is something fundamental and all-inclusive about time. Our lives as a whole, as well as all our activities, are bounded and shaped by time in a remarkably continuous and pervasive manner. Everything changes "in" time except time itself; that alone lies outside and beyond the ravage of time. Everything else, both the world we perceive as well as our own experience of ourselves, is formed and ordered by it. Philosophers from Plato to Hegel and Heidegger have recognized this, noting that time is something without which there could be nothing else. Indeed, in the history of philosophy it is probably fair to say that only one other concept—that of "Being" itself—has shared with time such a fundamental, pivotal, and all-important place. For Heidegger, for example, time is so fundamental as to be "the *perspective governing* the disclosure of being."[11] And for Kant, time is not only "an absolute primary, formal principle of the sensible world,"[12] but also the a priori structure of all consciousness and understanding itself. For Kant, time is not just another or even merely an important and significant reality; it is *the* fundamental and basic one! Without it there could be no perception, no "external" world, no scientific knowledge, no consciousness, no logic or thought, in fact no philosophy at all.

---

[10] Gerald E. Myers, *Self: An Introduction to Philosophical Psychology* (New York: Pegasus, 1969), p. 14.

[11] Martin Heidegger, *An Introduction to Metaphysics*, trans. Ralph Mannheim (New York: Doubleday, 1961), p. 172.

[12] Immanuel Kant, "Dissertation on the Form and Principles of the Sensible World," in Charles Sherover, *The Human Experience of Time* (New York: New York University Press, 1975), p. 149.

But there is another reason for exploring the nature of time before developing a philosophy of self. It seems rather evident that there has always been a very intimate connection between time and self. Any theory of the former seems to entail a conception of the latter and vice versa. That means that any conception of self rests upon and is deeply determined by the underlying and often assumed view of time which the analyst in question brings to his or her study. It seems fairly clear that Hume's notorious perplexity and confusion about the self is due in large part to his conception of time as a series of fragmented and unbridgeable moments. If the traditional views of self are so strongly influenced by their author's conception of time, then we might expect that a rather different philosophy of time will entail a radically altered notion of personal identity. That is in fact just what I hope to show.

One caution before we begin: as we have already indicated, this will be a phenomenological study. In other words, we are interested here in evoking and articulating the *experience* of self *to that self*. But that means we will have to try to set aside thinking in terms or categories more appropriate to *things* than *agents* in the "world" of ordinary experience. In fact, there seems to have been a rather overwhelming tendency in our tradition to do just that, to treat the self as a sort of static entity. Perhaps it is built right into our language, but one constantly detects reverberations in the literature on self which imply that "it" is a sort of thing-like being. For example, Hume seems frustrated in the *Treatise* in part because he can find no such thing-like self which endures over time as a sort of substantial identity, like a marble. Even as sophisticated a contemporary philosopher as Daniel Dennett can ask in all seriousness, "Where am I?"[13] meaning whether the "I" can be *located* like a thing in the body or in the brain. To me, doing that seems analogous to asking where "love" or "anxiety" are "located." At any rate, because it is a "substance" or "reality" and because, as Heidegger says, reality is often reduced to or understood in terms of object-entities present to consciousness, a self is assumed to be a sort of object-thing behind the flow of moments and is pictured as the subject which links the predicates we ascribe to "it." As Boethius put it, following Aristotle, a *person* is "an individual substance of a rational nature."[14]

But a self to itself, that is, from the point of view of its own experience, is neither an object of experience nor a kind of entity thing. "As things go, it is not one of them."[15] We will try to show that the nature of

---

[13] Daniel C. Dennett, "Where Am I?", in Douglas R. Hofstadter and Daniel C. Dennett, *The Mind's I* (New York: Basic Books, 1981), chap. 13.
[14] Quoted in John A. T. Robinson, *Exploration Into God* (Stanford: Stanford University Press, 1967), p. 10.
[15] Rorty, *Identities*, p. 13.

a self or person within the world of ordinary experience is tied up with the execution of intentional acts, with what he or she *does*. Such persons are not so much objects over or through time as they are *temporal relations* which shape and form those actions. Selves are not things "in" time, but temporal *processes* or *dynamic activities*. Selves are tensed. To treat them in terms of "things" or "objects" is to fall into a "category mistake."

> Ego, I, or self cannot be characterized at all in terms appropriate for objects. . . . And so we already have a vocabulary appropriate enough to its own sphere. In the literature of subjectivity characteristic terms are freedom rather than causation; intention rather than literal direction; the reflexive rather than the simple or immediate; meanings rather than causes; values rather than facts; negation rather than affirmation; and finally truth and honesty rather than propositional correctness.[16]

In what follows, we hope to show: (1) that most of what has been wrong with the traditional views of self can be traced back to an inadequate and incorrect view of time; (2) that a phenomenological analysis of time affords a corrective to such a view of time and thereby provides a fresh and interesting way to get at what it means to be a self or person; and finally (3) that the precipitous, traditional pendulum-swing between "empiricist" and "rationalist" notions of self, as Bergson puts it, *presupposes* as a condition for the possibility of either or both extreme the view of time and self which I will be trying to articulate here. That is, a self is neither a present atomic fragment which invents its own identity over time nor a transcendental unity above and beyond real succession and difference through time. Both these positions, I think, presuppose a temporal self which is a sort of third position, undercutting and making clear the sort of abstract, half-truth that each of the others is.

[16] Earle, *Autobiographical Consciousness*, p. 48.

Chapter Two
PHILOSOPHICAL ISSUES

'Who are You?' said the Caterpillar.

This was not an encouraging opening for a conversation. Alice replied, rather shyly, 'I—I hardly know, just at present—at least I know who I was when I got up this morning, but I think I must have been changed several times since then.'

'What do you mean by that?' said the Caterpillar sternly. 'Explain yourself!'

'I can't explain myself, I'm afraid, Sir,' said Alice, 'because I'm not myself, you see.'

'I don't see,' said the Caterpillar.
—Lewis Carroll, *Alice's Adventures in Wonderland*

The general problem of self we have been discussing so far can be subdivided into at least four further immensely perplexing issues, issues with which any adequate philosophy of self must come to grips. Before advancing our own view of the self, it might be helpful to briefly clarify and explore these issues so that we will have some idea of what we are trying to accomplish and resolve.

1. The Unity Question

Each person is the *same* person over time. How is that possible? How is it possible—as Alice tells the Caterpillar—that something which over time is very *different* from what it was before is yet the *same*? "What *unites* a person's present experiences with his past experiences?"[1] It is not just Alice who has a problem here; we all do. John Smith at thirteen years of age is *not* what he was at two nor what he will be at forty-five. His body (all of its cells), his feelings, his thoughts, his values, his sense of himself—all are different. Yet he and we bind those different persons into one, just this particular John Smith. The problem of the *unity* or *sameness* of a self over time is at once bound up with difference and distinctness, i.e., it is a unity which must bind together difference.

---

[1] Godfrey Vesey, *Personal Identity: A Philosophical Analysis* (Ithaca, NY: Cornell University Press, 1974), p. 7.

> It appears to be an inborn need of all men to regard the self as a
> unity. . . . In reality, however, every ego, so far from being a
> unity is in the highest degree a manifold world, a constellated
> heaven, a chaos of forms, of stages and stages, of inheritance and
> potentialities.[2]

In what follows, we shall claim that a self is *both* unity and difference,
and that those positions which reduce it either to a series of fragmented
moments or a transtemporal unity beyond change do so because of an
assumed notion of time and in spite of the phenomenological facts.

2. The Identity Issue

When I awake in the morning, I know I am "I" without recourse to
a comparison with myself seven hours or seven days earlier. Thus, my
identity—that which makes me "me," now or earlier—is not identical to
the question of unity or sameness over time. As John Perry puts it, "Simi-
larity, however exact, is not identity. I use identity to mean there is but
one thing."[3]

What are the characteristics which make of a particular person
exactly the person or self he or she is? John Locke answered this question
by locating the identity of self within present memory. Thus, the "I"
now and the "I" earlier are constituted as a kind of shadow or hindsight.
"Nothing but consciousness can unite remote existences into the same
person."[4] But that leads to a serious problem. As Anthony Quinton puts
it, "How is the identity through time of the supposed identifier to be
established?"[5] Thomas Reid, recognizing that Locke's position can hardly
account for that, takes the opposite tack.

> My personal identity, therefore, implies the continued existence of
> that indivisible thing which I call *myself*. Whatever self may be, it
> is something which thinks, and deliberates, and resolves, and acts,
> and suffers. I am not thought, I am not action, I am not feeling; I am
> something that thinks, and acts, and suffers. My thoughts, and
> actions, and feelings, change every moment; they have no contin-
> ued, but a successive, existence; but that *self*, or I, to which they
> belong, is permanent and has the same relation to all the succeeding
> thoughts, actions and feelings which I call mine.[6]

[2] Herman Hesse, *Steppenwolf*, trans. Basil Creighton (New York: Holt, Rinehart and
Winston, 1963), pp. 66–67.

[3] John Perry, *A Dialogue on Personal Identity and Immortality* (Indianapolis, IN:
Bobbs-Merrill, 1978), p. 6.

[4] John Locke, "Of Identity and Diversity," *Essay Concerning Human Understanding*,
in *Personal Identity*, ed. John Perry (Los Angeles: University of California Press, 1975), p.
48.

[5] Anthony Quinton, "The Soul," in Perry, *Personal Identity*, p. 55.

[6] Thomas Reid, "Of Identity," *Essays on the Intellectual Powers of Man*, in Perry, *Personal Identity*, p. 109.

At any rate, I think that my view of temporal action affords a way to get at this issue of *identity* which avoids the (by now) familiar horns of the dilemma represented here by Locke and Reid.

3. The Problem of Self-Deception

Imagine a typical psychotherapeutic event, in this case becoming conscious of an earlier repressed and unconscious feeling such as anger.

> I had earlier believed that I felt no anger when my friend betrayed me; but what I discovered later is that in fact I 'repressed' that anger, deceived myself into 'believing' that I did not really feel it while actually being very angry.

It is important to note that I am not learning a new psychological theory which might account for my depression or anxiety. On the contrary, what is going on here is my letting myself actually re-experience that old anger which I had not remembered until now. It is that "aha" experience of becoming aware of something which in some sense one "knew" all along. I do not learn a new theory, then, but come to discover or let myself realize both my earlier anger as well as my repression of it. Psychotherapy, at least in part, consists of just this sort of recall of apparent acts of self-deception in which "I" somehow manage both to forget and yet remember, believe and not believe at the same time. In other words, the very technique and efficacy of psychotherapy appears to rest upon our ability to deceive ourselves. But how is that possible?

Self-deception actually seems radically impossible since it apparently violates the law of noncontradiction.[7] If I deceive myself, I seem both to believe (x) and not believe (-x) at the same time and in the same way. "I" (the deceiver) hold one thing and "I" (the deceived) hold another. Now that would be just fine if the two selves were different. In that case there would be no contradiction since in fact there would be two separate and distinct selves (deceiver and deceived). But there is a cost to this solution. By breaking the act of deception into two separate selves, we indeed solve the problem of contradiction, but only by doing away with the *self*-deception. If "I" am ignorant, "I" am not *self*-deceived.

Self-deception seems to entail a single self which deceives itself. But there is a cost to that, too, as we have seen; namely that such a self enters into contradiction by holding *both* x and -x. To maintain the self-deception, we *must* have a single self over the act of self-deception, but that leads us to the apparent absurdity of a self which both knows and does not know at the same time. And as if that were not bad enough, we

---

[7] Much of what follows here, including the notion of a "dialectical solution," comes from a hitherto unpublished essay by Neil Weiner entitled, "Self-Deception, The Unconscious, and the Divided Self."

run head on into another dilemma. If the self actually *does* know, then it is not self-deceived. If it does *not* know, then it is ignorant and likewise not self-deceived. In either case, self-deception seems impossible.

But that is absurd! As we noted in our example, we actually *experience* our own self-deception. How is this possible? What we need is a conception of the self which can carry us between the horns of this dilemma: *either* self-deception involves two distinct selves (deceiver and deceived or "I" and a "demon" within me) which then obliterates the self-deception in favor of a plain old-fashioned deception of one self by another; *or* a single self (both deceiver and deceived) which embraces its responsibility by holding contradictory opinions at the same time and in the same way. We need an understanding of self which comes in between these vicious horns, a conception which is dialectical in that it takes from the first alternative in the dilemma the view that there is real *difference* between the deceiver and the deceived; while at the same time taking from the second the notion that there is a *unity* which binds those different selves into a single and self-deceived "I."

It is just that sort of dialectical understanding of self which we will be proposing in Part Three, a notion which will permit us to affirm and understand self-deception while avoiding blatant acts of logical contradiction to maintain and explain it.

4. The Problem of Attitude

Of the many remarkable and unique aspects of persons or selves, perhaps the most extraordinary lies in the apparent fact that a self is fundamentally tied up with his or her *attitude* toward life or life-value. For example, as opposed to Stalin, what made Gandhi precisely the person he was had something to do with Gandhi's basic attitude and sense of what life is all about. Indeed, if he had changed that attitude, he would no longer be precisely the Gandhi we have come to know, but another person.

When and if we change or modify ourselves, we do so by changing our fundamental attitudes about our lives and selves. "Humans are just the sorts of organisms that interpret and modify their agency through their conception of themselves."[8] As Heidegger might put it, a self is not a "substance"-like-thing that just *is* whatever it happens to be, but a kind of reality for which "Being is an issue" and which becomes what its sense or "understanding" of the meaning of Being is.[9] But how can this be the case? What kind of a reality must this self or person be to be able to actualize itself in terms of its own attitude about itself and life in general?

[8] Rorty, *Identities*, p. 323.
[9] Martin Heidegger, *Being and Time*, trans. John Macquarrie and Edward Robinson (New York: Harper & Row, 1962), p. 32.

Clearly, our path is strewn with difficulties. I shall return to these specific issues in the last chapter, for any serious phenomenological study of self must not only develop a theory, but show how that theory helps to resolve or at least "dissolve" the puzzles and perplexities which in part helped to generate it. In the meantime, we will discuss a few of the "temporal conditions of self" in the next section, conditions which are prerequisite to any adequate phenomenological approach to personal identity.

PART TWO:
EXPLORING THE TEMPORAL
CONDITIONS OF SELF

Chapter Three
ACTION AND TIME

In the beginning was the act.
—Goethe, *Faust*

Action

Jacob Bronowski, in his fascinating survey of the evolution of human culture and mind, *The Ascent of Man*, asks himself, at one point, what it is that most distinguishes man from his near relations on the ladder of evolution. Is it the thumb? The brain? Perhaps it is his erect posture, or a significant chemical difference? No. These are differences, of course, but for Bronowski they are not the fundamental or key differences which enable us to understand the emergence of culture, human social patterns, art, science, and the life of the human mind in general. The real distinction, he goes on to say, lies in man's *activity*. Man is first and foremost the active or doing creature—*homo agens*.

Stuart Hampshire, in *Thought and Action*, shares Bronowski's sense of the primacy of action in human life when he distinguishes between perceptual observation and active engagement in the world.

> We are in the world, as bodies among bodies, not only as observers but as active experimenters. . . . In handling and manipulating, we are not so much perceiving as acting. . . . I find myself from the beginning able to act.[1]

Far from being "observers," who spend most of their time first sensing and perceiving the world and only then acting within it, as the eighteenth century philosophers tended to see us, it would seem on the contrary that we are fundamentally active and bodily beings at work in the world, and only secondarily and subordinately, perceivers and observers.

However that may be, it seems clear that this human activity is different than the activity of other animals, for we act *consciously* and *purposefully*. We can delay the gratification of our needs by acting toward future goals. In the case of a pole-vaulter, for example:

> The athlete is an adult whose behavior is not driven by his immediate environment, as animal actions are. In themselves, his

---

[1] Stuart Hampshire, *Thought and Action* (New York: The Viking Press, 1967), p. 53.

actions make no practical sense at all; they are an exercise not
directed to the present. The athlete's mind is fixed ahead of him,
building up his skill; and he vaults in imagination into the
future.[2]

In our action and behavior we are distinguished from other animals by
our ability to anticipate, to live and act toward distant goals rather than
being manipulated and controlled by our immediate surroundings.
Because we can anticipate such distant goals, we can visualize and imagine a future and plan to anticipate it in our art and science. We humans
are dreamers, and it is this ability to live out ahead of ourselves in our
actions that distinguishes us in the chain of evolution and which permits
us to develop mathematics, music, literature, biology, formal education,
and philosophy. For human beings, life is not so much a "something" as
an "opportunity" for something.

Human actions are pervaded by a unique sense of time, then; not in
some abstract way, nor in terms of the measurement of time by clocks
and calendars of various sorts. That is unique too, but a later development which presupposes the more original temporal sense we are trying
to characterize. The unique sense of time we are pointing to here is the
fact that human activity is a reaching out of the past and present toward
anticipated goals. Action is not "in" time nearly as much as it embodies
the movement of time itself![3] Putting it another way, we can no more
understand an action outside the horizon of the flow and dimensions of
time than we can understand breathing without oxygen and lungs.
Time—the flow or movement itself—is a necessary condition of our
behavior and lives.

I shall mean by "action," here, specifically human "doings" as
opposed to merely natural "events." A hurricane, the reaction of one
billiard ball striking another, and the descent of a falling weight from an
airplane are all examples of "events;" whereas getting on a bus, going to
college, and throwing oneself out of an airplane are typical kinds of
"action." "Action" involves the producing of something, a conscious or
preconscious doing which brings about an end or goal. What is "done" is
different from what simply "happens"—i.e., "actions" are not "events,"
although of course I want to emphasize that human actions are always
accompanied by, and meshed together with, "events." There are no dis-
embodied, unsituated, purely anticipatory human "actions." Therefore,
throwing oneself out of an airplane (an action) clearly involves and presupposes a series of events as a precondition: the person's heart continues
to beat and he goes on breathing; his body moves after he has set it in

---

[2] Jacob Bronowski, *The Ascent of Man* (Boston: Little, Brown, 1973), p. 36.

[3] Surprisingly enough, that is just what Plotinus held: "Time is the form of activity of
purposive life" (Plotinus, *Enneads*, in Sherover, *Human Experience of Time*, p. 32).

motion and, once outside the airplane, it falls. As John MacMurray has put it:

> We understand what is done by reference to the intention of an agent. What merely happens we refer to another happening which we call its cause. Actions are the realization of intentions; events the effects of causes.[4]

All right, let us take a brief look at a typical set of actions from the "inside" as it were, as the agent lives them through. Not only will this help to plunge us back into our ordinary experience so that we may focus upon it, but eventually we will try to unpack or verbally make evident the temporal structure of just such lived actions. I had just left my office to go to class when Neil ran up to me in the corridor and said, "You have an emergency phone call, Paul, from the hospital." I rushed back to my office, jammed the key into the lock, and swung the door open as I turned the key. In two strides I was over to the phone. "Oh, no!" I thought to myself. "Oh, damn!" As I reached for the phone, I thought of the peacefulness I had felt just before as I had set out along the corridor toward my class. My mind had been occupied with Augustine's conception of sin . . . but all that was gone now. I reached for the phone with my heart in my mouth as I dialed the hospital. "Hello! Hello!"

Now, what can we say about such action? First of all, we should note carefully that actions as we live them through are never experienced as isolated, self-contained, or fragmented. On the contrary, they always and inevitably refer to actions which precede them and to anticipated goals which they "seek" or reach toward. "Walking along the corridor," for example, implies within itself having just left my office, closed the door, turned up the corridor; and of course the very act of walking along the corridor also anticipates or reaches toward getting to the classroom, and so on. The same kind of matrix is true of "putting the key in the lock," "reaching for the phone," "recalling how I felt earlier," and in fact *any* action as the agent lives or acts it through. Actions are always situated in a halo or horizon of past actions which fall off behind them and anticipated goals which they intend. I do not normally *think* about these past actions and anticipated goals, although as we will see more clearly later, I *can* do that; rather, I simply act, and the action implicitly contains what we will call a "coreference" to them which situates it. In other

---

[4] John MacMurray, *Persons in Relation* (New York: Harper and Brothers, 1961), p. 221. Also, see T. Parsons and E. A. Shils, eds., *Toward a General Theory of Action* (Cambridge, MA: Harvard University Press, 1951), p. 34; C. Taylor, *The Explanation of Behavior* (London: Routledge and Kegan Paul, 1964), p. 8; R. S. Peters, *The Concept of Motivation* (London: Routledge and Kegan Paul, 1958), pp. 4ff; and Allan R. White, *Introduction to the Philosophy of Action* (London: Oxford University Press, 1968), p. 2.

words, my actions are a sort of emergence out of what I was just doing
and a reaching toward anticipated ends, and I am implicitly aware of
that in the doing itself.

Temporality

Temporality is the very *form* of doing, the structure of action. When
we act, we act in a context, that is with just this past "behind" and just
those goals out "ahead." Our actions are or contain a sort of *temporal
relation* of the past to the future. The anticipation and the conditionality
of our actions do not emerge from explicit memory and conscious visualization of the future, as if we existed and acted merely in an atomic and
isolated present. That is a common enough misconception of time. Aside
from other problems, that would make action meaningless by disintegrating it into discrete fragments which would never add up over time
to the interconnected *flow* it actually and necessarily is. Rather, that
existing and acting temporally, that going beyond what has been toward
what might be, that eruption out of conditions into possibility, that
bridge-over is the *sine quâ non* for *conscious* recall of the past and *explicit* visualization of the future. *They* are possible precisely because we are
already aware in our ordinary and preconceptual lives and actions of
what it means to have a past (to exist "pastly," I want to say) and to live
toward anticipated goals (to act "anticipatorily").

> If I know that I am doing something, then I know *ipso facto* the
> distinction between past and future which is the form of doing.
> To be aware of what I am doing while doing it is to be aware at
> once both of what I have already done and of what I have yet to
> do.[5]

But it is not just that actions in general manifest time in the sense of
a temporal "flow." They also reveal in themselves the "dimensionality,"
"seriality," and "continuity" of time; and it is through our actions that we
become "aware" of time and "measure" it with various kinds of clocks.
Indeed, the analysis of our temporal activity provides a means to come
to grips with all of the traditional philosophical issues of time. Through
reflection we discover our lives in midstream. We discover that we have
already been acting, and by that means we can become conscious of
these elements of time. For instance, in our example, I was going to my
class "before" Neil stopped me in the corridor to tell me about the emergency phone call. I "was" going to class and thinking about Augustine's
notion of sin; that was followed by a new "present" in which I rushed to
my office to call the hospital. "After" talking to Neil but "before" tele-
phoning the hospital, I unlocked and opened the door and rushed to the

---

[5] John MacMurray, *The Self As Agent* (New York: Harper and Brothers, 1957), p. 169.

phone. As I reached for the phone, the act of jamming the key in the door was still stinging my hand and Neil's look and words were just "behind" me, the past I had just gone beyond in order to telephone the hospital. The living-through of acting, the *doing* in which I was involved, is a kind of preconceptual experience which is or contains that temporal sense within it. I already "know" the "flow," the "dimensionality," the "seriality," and "continuity" of time *before* I consciously think about them because they are part of my ordinary actions. To act is by that very fact already to know what time is, and the bringing of time to conscious articulation is nothing but a bringing of the temporal horizon of our ordinary actions to consciousness by reflecting upon those lived actions.

Let us do that, then. Let us take a closer look at temporality or the temporal relation, for our later anlysis and understanding of self and personal identity will rest upon it.

Chapter Four

THE TEMPORAL RELATION

My heart beating, my blood running,
The light brimming,
My mind moving, the ground turning,
My eyes blinking, the air flowing,
The clock's quick-ticking,
Time moving, time dying,
Time perpetually perishing!
Time is farewell! Time is farewell!
—Delmore Schwartz, from "Time's Dedication"

The Dimensions of Temporality

There is a "form" of separation or *dimensionality* about all temporal experience, namely the division of time into present, past, and future. We can *imagine* a time in which we are not involved, a time characterized simply in terms of a series of events arranged in order of succession like beads on a string. But as soon as we introduce *ourselves* into time or as soon as we focus upon our actual temporal experience, the dimensions of past, present, and future emerge and fundamentally qualify that temporal experience. Because of this, I am always located in a "now," the present. That "now," however, leads beyond itself to future, anticipated events which are "not yet" and looks back to past events which are "no longer." As Aristotle realized, "now" is both unchanging (I am invariably located within "now") and the shifting link between the past and future (the present "now" is not the earlier one).[1]

1. The Eternal Now

As we saw in the last chapter, experientially we are always "situated" in terms of our activity, located in relation to what we *are* doing, *have been* doing, and *intend* to do. For example, "I am presently sitting at my desk writing. Until a few minutes ago, I had been reading an article; before that, I ate lunch with my wife. What I want to do is finish enough writing today so that I can round off this section of the essay by the end of this week."

---

[1] Aristotle, "Physics," in *The Basic Works of Aristotle*, ed. R. McKeon (New York: Random House, 1941), p. 219:13ff.

We must not conceive of a present "now" as a sort of bead on a thread, accidentally related to the "now" instants which precede and follow it. The present is never given to me as a point, but always as an ensemble defined in terms of a given situation. "Now" is neither an instant nor essentially unrelated to those preceding and following "nows." In forcing our attention back into the context of our active, bodily experience in the world, we will find that "now" signals an extension of varying length within a total biography.

"Now" is a function of our actions. Because of this, the nature and "extension" of the "now" varies directly in proportion to the situation in which we find ourselves involved. "I am now writing in my study, whereas before I was eating my lunch. The reason I am writing is in order to finish this essay. In pursuit of that goal, I put aside the article I had been reading, sharpened my pencils, and started to write. . . ." A "now," including the present "now," is *not* defined in terms of a series of measured instants (the ticking of a clock, for example) but rather is a *situation* defined in terms of the functions or activities in which I or we are engaged.

"Now" can mean almost an infinitely large extension of time or a mere instant. Consider, for example, the following: "Before creation, there was nothing; *now*, there is *being* in all of its infinite majesty." Or consider, "Prepare for ignition: five . . . four . . . three . . . two . . . one . . . *now*." In the former case, the now is defined in terms of mental contemplation of "being;" in the latter, it is stipulated in terms of our counting the movement of a second hand as a function of a familiar technological situation. The character of any "now" varies according to the situation in which we find ourselves involved.

The doings or activities which situate my experience and define "now" vary, of course, from perception to contemplation of ideas, to bodily exertions, to recall of past "nows." Since each "now" is defined in terms of what we *do*, then new "nows" emerge when we turn to new activities. "I am writing. I am *now* recalling that day at my office when the hospital telephoned to tell me that my daughter was in the emergency room after an automobile accident. Actually (now), I am recalling being in the corridor on the way to class just *before* the telephone call. No, I am remembering (now) that I had been thinking about Augustine's conception of sin. . . ." The shift from writing to recall defines a new "now" and shoves the former one (writing) into the past. In the same way, each successive act of recall situates and separates a series of nows which emerge with them.

The present "now," therefore, is first felt as a field of endeavor, a situation, an horizon in which we lead our active lives. "The present is that which is contemporaneous with my activity."[2] Having set out to write a book, for example, I move toward that goal by engaging in activities which seek to accomplish it: I actively turn toward new acts, thereby passing by the former act and making a new one present. I sharpen my pencils, then I set the paper, adjust the light, arrange my notes, and begin to write. A present "now" is a situation in which I am actively involved—with others or alone—and *using* the world around me to help me accomplish the goals of my actions. I do not so much "perceive" my pencil as *use* it to write.[3]

It is essential to realize that a "now," just like the activity which determines and delineates it, cannot be understood as an isolated and purely discrete instant. On the contrary, each "now" must be seen within the horizon of the retained past and the anticipated future. My activity "now" is "now" only against the background of former and anticipated "nows." Being "now" at the desk is fundamentally related to having earlier come into the room and sat down and to the intended goal of finishing another section of writing. Consequently, the present "now" is carved out of a biography *in process*, as an aspect of it. Each action is a process of doing which takes place and makes sense only in the context of immediate and more distant past activities and over against the anticipated goals which the action seeks.

The present is a sort of horizon of activity in which the very sense of being "present" involves an immediate past and future. What I am doing is the result of what I did before, and it points to what I will do later. It is not so much that I explicitly recall the past or explicitly envisage the future, although I can do that. Rather, I seem to have them in hand and their immediacy bears upon my action "now." I read the page of the book, having just opened it, and in order to find that special reference I need. The passing of the present refers to an anticipated action, finding the quote which then becomes present, shoving the former "now" into the immediately retained past. My present fulfills the immediate past's intentions and intends a yet-to-be-fulfilled future state. Having opened the book, it is open and I am reading it in order to discover the yet-to-be-found quote, which may or may not be fulfilled later. "A now-phase is thus added only as a boundary of a continuity of retentions."[4]

---

[2] Paul Fraise, *The Psychology of Time*, trans. J. Leith (London: Eyre and Spottiswoode, 1964), p. 84.

[3] Maurice Merleau-Ponty, *Phenomenology of Perception*, trans. Colin Smith (New York: Humanities Press, 1962), p. 416.

[4] Edmund Husserl, *The Phenomenology of Internal Time Consciousness*, ed. Martin Heidegger, trans. J. S. Churchill (Bloomington: Indiana University Press, 1964), p. 55.

2. Retention

The past is that which "already has been." It has been but is no longer present. Thus, the past is made up of a series of no longer present situations which have been passed by when a new "now" is made present. A while ago I was eating lunch; then I came up to my study to write and our pleasant lunch slipped into the past.

Just as a present "now" is a function of our active doings, the past is defined negatively in terms of what we are not or no longer doing. A past "now" is a situation or activity in which we *were* but *are no longer* engaged.

The immediate past is what has just been. As we have already indicated, it is retained as the immediate horizon of my present activity or situation. For example, having just sharpened my pencils and arranged the paper, I begin to write. . . . We have the past "in hand" as the immediate context for our present activity. "We feel it behind us as an incontestable acquisition."[5]

Retentions, then, are *not* consciously recalled, but are the context of "already-having-been-ness" which, along with anticipation, enfold the present situation and are the existential basis for explicit recall. We are not conscious of the retained past any more than we are necessarily conscious of what our actions anticipate or intend. Retentions are simply the felt "already-having-been-ness" of actions, as for example, the "smooth" and "cool" feel of the paper between my fingers as I arrange it on my desk in order to write. I do not recall that paper (although I *can* do that) nearly as much as let it bear upon my present activity as the immediate context of it. It is back there, ready for recall, but preconsciously forming or shaping and situating my present action. The retained past is not present, but weighs upon it as an horizon of it.

Recall, on the other hand, is a *present* and *conscious* activity. Recall is an activity, a doing which like any other defines a present situation. For example, "I was talking with Neil when I suddenly recalled that we had discussed this before. I lost myself in the remembrance of that earlier conversation and no longer heard Neil talking to me. . . ." Recall is an activity which takes place in or defines the present. It makes the retained, unconscious past present in image form, meaning by "image" here not a "copy" or "facsimile" but a perspective upon the retained past. My having lunch and then coming to my study to write lies back there as a retained horizon or halo of my present activity of writing. But I *can* consciously recall it, the soup and sandwich, the table with a vase of flowers, the conversation. When I do make a retained past "present," I recall it. I "see" the lunch from here or from over there; I "taste" it or

---

[5] Merleau-Ponty, *Phenomenology of Perception*, p. 414.

"smell" it in the explicit act of recall. The "images" *through* which I recall the past are perspectives on the past and intentionally refer beyond themselves to the retained past event.

Interestingly enough, the conscious act of making it *present* by means of recall makes the retained past consciously *"past"* for the first time. The "past" after all can only be "past" for a "present"; before that, the retention is neither "past" nor "present," but, as we have said, the context of "already-having-been-ness" which helps to circumscribe present activity.

When we turn to new activities, we make present a new "now" aimed at an anticipated or intended goal. For example, we were tired of playing squash so we left the squashcourt and headed for the showers. "That was great," my friend said, "but I'm really looking forward to a shower." Making present a new "now" shoves the former "now" from the present into the past. The whole series of retained events are shoved back, gradually sinking into obscurity and remoteness and having little bearing upon present acts and situations.

As we have seen, a present situation must be seen in the context of an horizon of retentions and anticipations. Past "nows" retain that contextuality with what we call their "coreference" to past retentions which anticipate them (and which they fulfill) and later retentions which they anticipate and which fulfill them. "I recall coming into my study. I was going to sharpen my pencils and then write. I had just finished my lunch so that I could get back to writing." Although each past "now" is discrete and separate from any other ("lunch" was not and never will be "sharpening pencils"), *there is a "coreferentiality" about each retained situation which arises from the contextual character of present activity with its horizon of retentions and anticipations.* Each "now," along with its anticipations and retentions, gets retained as such. That means that there are retentions of retentions (what Husserl called the "running-off" phenomenon)[6] and that each retention is the locus of a coreferentiality of past retentions and future anticipations. Like the present, a past "now" is never an isolated bead on a string: it always takes place in a total biography, in a set of coreferential relations which reach through actions and bridge time with continuity.

3. Anticipation

Just as retention is a preconscious halo of "already-having-been-ness," *anticipation* is the preconscious intentionality of our actions, the "not-yet-ness," "lack," or "possibility" toward which any action reaches.

Let us imagine that I find myself in a boxing ring. The bell for

[6] Husserl, *Internal Time Consciousness*, p. 49.

round one has just sounded and I grope through the surrounding clamor to encounter my adversary. As we eye one another behind our gloved shields and circle about, each searches out openings in the other. Suddenly, his left shoots out toward my face. As it does, I move my body to block it by shifting my weight onto my right foot and lifting my right glove. As I deflect the blow, I shift my weight to the left and swing toward his open stomach with my left hand.

In this situation, and indeed in any such continuous act, we can find the original sense of anticipation. My body acts toward certain intended ends, indeed I am a certain lack of the anticipated goal which my bodily actions seek to accomplish. As he swings, I act to fill in the lack, I protect myself before the immediately anticipated blow to my face. When I see an opening, I *act* to fill it. I move toward an anticipated state with my body, a left to his belly.

Part of the context of any activity, then, is this state of anticipation. For example, in stepping off a bus, I reach *toward* the sidewalk, I move toward it, I gain it. These anticipated states are sometimes near, sometimes far. Thus, my stepping out of a bus to reach the sidewalk is an immediate goal toward which I act. It is an intermediate step toward reaching the more distant goal of arriving at home.

Like retention, anticipation is *not* a conscious act as such. I move toward the sidewalk from the bus or I swing toward my adversary without consciously envisaging a goal, although I *can* do that if I choose. However, if I do that while boxing, I will have stopped boxing to "*imagine*" the future instead. Rather, acting toward an end is part of the horizon of any concrete action, a lack which I feel and which impinges upon and helps to define that situation.

We must not conceive of this state of being as a "present" construction of possible states in the future. First of all, the state of anticipation is not itself "present" insofar as it is not conscious. Secondly, we could never construct "futurity" from simply "present" elements.

> Even if, *per impossible*, I could construct consciousness of the past with transferred presents, they certainly could not open a future for me. . . . How could one anticipate if one had no sense of the future.[7]

In fact, the sense of anticipation does not in any sense resemble a *present* construction of a possible future state. We sense it, feel it out ahead, because, as we have seen, we exist ahead of ourselves toward possible being in our actions.

> Projecting has nothing to do with comporting oneself toward a plan that has been thought out and in accordance with which Dasein

---

[7] Merleau-Ponty, *Phenomenology of Perception*, p. 414.

arranges its Being. On the contrary, any Dasein has, as Dasein, already projected itself; and as long as it is, it is projecting.[8]

We do not mean by anticipation a "future" now which has not yet become actual but will be sometime later. Rather, we are talking here of the existential condition for such a notion of "futurity." As with the "past," there can be no "future" except to and for a "present." We mean that aspect of our actions which is "possible," at issue, and in relation to which I am now a lack. My being is not simply "present"; I also exist as "already-having-been" and as a kind of anticipation, out "ahead" of my present as a lack which I act to overcome. Before joining the army, for example, I am related to it as possibility, and I act toward it in my present and over against my past: I flee the country or I take a bus to the induction center. After I join, then the "joining" is retained, i.e., I have already been "joined" to it—it is finished, done with. Anticipation is an aspect of my being in which what I will be and do is "open," at issue; and I act toward that as a *lack* of it.

Anticipation is like retention insofar as it is a preconscious and original part of the horizon or context of any action. But unlike retention, which involves "already-having-been-ness," anticipation refers to what is "not yet" or "possible" being. Whereas there is a certain determinateness and fixity to retention, anticipations are "empty." They *are* not yet. While retention entails a certain closedness, or givenness and irrevocability, anticipation is exactly the opposite; it is characterized by a certain openness, a not-yet-having-been decided or actualized.

Furthermore, retention and anticipation vary in terms of their fulfillment, and that is essential to their natures. Thus, retention is *recalled* and consciously discovered to be "past" through that recollection. Anticipations are fulfilled in terms of *expectation* and *consciously* discovered to be "future" within such expectation. Retention is the condition for recall implicit within that recall. Anticipation, on the other hand, is the condition for expectation and is implicit within that. Whereas retentions are merely followed by further retentions, anticipations are what Husserl calls "about to be perceived" and thus are followed by and accomplished in present perceptions. Lastly, retentions sink back in the past, whereas anticipations are only vaguely and loosely interrelated "out ahead."

Both retention and anticipation, therefore, are original aspects of our actions and experience and both provide the condition for the conscious emergence of the temporal dimensions of "past" and "future." "Expectational intuition is something primordial and unique exactly as is intuition of the past"[9] We can "know" the past and we can image the future because in our very *acting* we are temporal per se.

---

[8] Heidegger, *Being and Time*, p. 185.
[9] Husserl, *Internal Time Conscousness*, p. 81.

In walking through a forest, I move my body toward anticipated states and ends. For example, I edge around a huge boulder to get to the path on the other side, I lift my hand to remove the branch that is about to strike my face. All of this I do unconsciously. But if I should want to, I *can* envisage the anticipated goals of my actions. I can stop on the forest path and imagine the trail which is just out of sight, smell the pine grove I imagine up the hill. Tired and dry, I not only anticipate the waterfall I hear up ahead by walking toward it while loosening my canteen, but I can envisage it as well by *imagining* it across my anticipation, by "seeing" how it will look, "feeling" its cool wetness, "tasting" its freshness in the back of my mouth.

Thus, within "expectation" we *consciously* "anticipate" or imagine an anticipated state toward which we can *act*. As Husserl puts it, "In expectation phantasy forms the idea of the future from the past."[10] Like recall in relation to retention, expectation involves images which are *of* an anticipated state, which intend that state. Thus, we "see" the future through our images *of* it. But unlike recall, the components of our images of the anticipated future are constructed out of our experience of the past. For example, the trail I envisage around the corner is "like" many trails I have seen before. Furthermore, since the anticipations are consistent lines of intentionality from the present, i.e., fulfillments of past and present acts, then our images of that future flow from and are consistent with our past and present experience. The very act of envisaging a future act or event entails an intentional reference beyond it to the anticipated preconscious state. My images of possible being are over against the background of my existential lacks and possible being. I "see" the future through my images of it, but those images are not identical to it. They are perspectives upon it, images *of* it. This intentional reference within expectational consciousness helps to distinguish it from plain fantasy.

Retentions and anticipations exist as a sort of halo of my present activity, some close by and others more distant. Quâ retention and anticipation, they are felt rather than recalled or specifically envisaged or expected, grasped as bearing upon my present activity as the horizon and context of it. Over against the retained past, I make present new acts aimed at anticipated goals, thereby pushing the former "now" and the whole series of retentions into the past. "Temporality temporalizes itself as a future which makes present in the process of having-been."[11]

As we have seen, the "past" emerges from the *present* recall of a preconscious retention or series of retentions. And the "future" emerges from the *present* conscious "expectation" of an anticipated state toward which our actions reach. Neither retention nor anticipation, strictly

[10] Husserl, *Internal Time Consciousness*, p. 33.
[11] Heidegger, *Being and Time*, p. 401.

speaking, can be said to be "in" time or even dimensions or elements "of" time. Rather, they form the preconscious and experiential horizon or context of activity which is the necessary condition *for* time, the explicit dimensions of time (past, present, future) and the awareness of time. As Heidegger might put it, they are not "in" time but are the temporal "ecstasies" of *Dasein* which are the basis for "world time." In our terms, temporality (retention, making present, and anticipation) is the shape or form of action which makes "time" possible.

Succession

Any adequate philosophical analysis of time must come to grips with what Kant called the "order" of time, namely the phenomenon of *succession*. Without a succession of temporal moments, without "before" and "after," there is no time. There is about time an unchanging and a priori order of succession into which both experience and the objects of experience fall and thereby become temporally qualified. "All objects of the senses are in time and necessarily stand in time relations"[12] precisely because they fall within the order of succession which characterizes time.

In the process of making present toward anticipated ends, I shove back former "nows." The disengagement from one activity and the turning toward another provides us with the primitive phenomenon of "seriality" or succession. For example, if I should want to build a campfire, I collect stones for the fireplace, I gather twigs, then some dry grass, then I pile it all together, etc. As I move toward anticipated goals, I pass by or through a series of "nows" which are arranged serially, and retained as such.

A succession of events, however, is not the same thing as a *conception* or *awareness* of that succession, as William James has put it.[13] We become *aware* of succession through recall of the retained series because "succession" is itself retained and thus available for conscious recall.

Thus, when I am lighting the fire, I retain *in order* the series of successive events which have led to this present situation. Collecting the stones is not the same as piling the twigs or lighting the match. Each of the retained events, then, is successive and discrete, *not* what was before or after. But if each retained event is separate from the others, it is also essentially *related* to the others. Gathering the stones, piling the twigs,

---

[12] Kant, *Critique of Pure Reason*, trans. N. K. Smith (London: MacMillan and Co. Ltd., 1956), p. 77. Also, see Isaac Newton, "Scholium to the Definitions of the Mathematical Principles of Natural Philosophy," in J. J. C. Smart, ed., *Problems of Space and Time* (New York: The MacMillan Co., 1964), p. 83.

[13] William James, *The Principles of Psychology* (Chicago: Encyclopedia Britannica, 1952), p. 411.

lighting the match, all of this is part of building a campfire, and both the seriality and the "coreferentiality" are retained.

The relation of succession (before and after) remains irreversible. That I piled the twigs before I lit the campfire is as much an eternal fact of time as the fact that Robespierre died before Napoleon. The successive order of events in time remains fixed; we know that by simply recalling the succession of events we have retained.

Continuity

But, having shown succession or seriality in time is only half the story. For if there were no *continuity* through time, we would not have time at all, but sheer *difference* and thus constant creation.[14] On the other hand, if there were no *difference* in time (succession), there would be stasis and time willy-nilly would become eternity. As Samuel Alexander recognized, both succession (difference) and continuity (identity) seem to be essential characteristics of time.[15]

Various philosophies of time have divided on just this point, some emphasizing the continuity of time to the exclusion of real difference and some asserting just the opposite in a traditional dispute going back at least as far as Heraclitus and Parmenides.[16] Sartre expresses the problem most succinctly when he writes:

> If we first posit temporal unity, we risk no longer being able to understand anything about irreversible succession as the meaning of this unity, and if we consider the disintegrating succession as the original character of time, we risk no longer being able to understand that there is *one* time. If then there is no priority of unity over multiplicity, nor of multiplicity over unity, it is necessary to conceive of temporality as a unity which multiplies itself.[17]

[14] This was in effect the difficulty Descartes faced and recognized when he conceived of time as a series of isolated and unconnected moments. This led him to worry about personal identity over the gaps as well as continuity in creation ("substance"); and he came to feel—in large measure *because* of his view of time as a series of discrete atoms—that only God could guarantee continuity by His constant creation every moment. See Renè Descartes, "Meditations on First Philosophy," in *The Philosophical Works of Descartes*, trans. E. S. Haldane and G. R. T. Ross (New York: Dover Publications, 1968), vol. 1, p. 168, and "Arguments Demonstrating the Existence of God" (Addendum to Reply to Objection II), Axiom II, vol. 2, p. 56.

[15] Samuel Alexander, *Space, Time and Deity* (New York: Humanities Press, 1950), vol. 1, p. 45.

[16] For example, see Kant, *Critique of Pure Reason*, pp. 214ff., 217; F. H. Bradley, *Appearance and Reality* (Oxford: Oxford University Press, 1930), chaps. 4 and 5; John Locke, *The Works of John Locke* (London: Printed for Thomas Teg et. al., 1823), vol. 1, pp. 175ff., 191ff.; and Hume, *Treatise*, pp. 31ff., 37ff.

[17] Jean-Paul Sartre, *Being and Nothingness*, trans. H. Barnes (New York: Philosophical Library, 1956), p. 136.

As we have seen, successiveness is retained and thus discernible or knowable through conscious recall. But temporal activity also constitutes a continuity or unity. It is an ensemble of relations which mutually imply one another. Each "before" implies an "after," and vice versa. And each "now" is the "now" of this formerly and this later, and this formerly and later are over against this particular "now." The order of succession (before and after) as well as the dimensions of time are unthinkable unless they are interrelated with one another.

And just as with succession, we can "see" this continuity or unity within the successive and serially retained "nows." As we say, each "now" exists as an horizon of presence, retention, and anticipation, and *the entire horizon is retained.* Rather than a simple series of unrelated links in a chain, the retentions all refer beyond themselves (just as does present activity, of which they are retentions) in what we have called "coreferentiality" to what precedes and what follows. Thus we find a continuity stretching right through the successively retained "nows," a continuity which links each moment and which makes a set of retentions "mine." "Time is not a line, but a network of intentionalities."[18] Or as Husserl describes the same phenomenon:

> With regard to the running-off phenomenon, we know that it is a continuity of constant transformations which form an inseparable unity, not severable into parts which could be by themselves nor divisible into phases, parts of the continuity, which could be by themselves. The parts which by a process of abstraction we can throw into relief can only exist in the entire running-off.[19]

Each "now" is a continuity of retained and anticipated modifications. The unity of our actions is a breachless unity, but it is that only over against the real separation and difference of the successive moments and dimensions of time. The parts of time are "parts" only over against the whole; while that whole is a whole only by reaching over or through the parts. As Bergson puts it, "There is a succession of states, each of which announces that which follows and contains that which precedes it."[20] Human action is a flow which contains both continuity and difference, a self-anticipating movement which never leaves itself.

The Flow of Time

But having dealt with the dimensions, succession, and continuity of time, we still are not finished with our temporal analysis of action. We must also come to grips with the *flow* or movement of time, what has been traditionally referred to as the "course" of time. It is here that we

[18] Merleau-Ponty, *Phenomenonology of Perception*, p. 417.
[19] Husserl, *Internal Time Consciousness*, p. 48.
[20] Bergson, *Metaphysics*, p. 11.

come across the familiar image of time as a flowing stream.

> Time is a river of things that become, with a strong current. No
> sooner is a thing seen than it has been swept away, and some-
> thing else is being carried past, and still another thing will
> follow.[21]

If we did not have a flow or movement of events in time, we would not
be dealing with time at all, but with eternity.[22] That which is past
becomes more past, the present becomes past, the future present, and the
distant future less future. There is a motion, therefore, which—carrying
the successive events on its back and structured by the dimensional form
of time—reaches throughout the extent of time. One thing is not temporal, and that is time itself! Time never stops. Events flow from the distant future toward the distant past. The direction of the flow seems fixed
and yet, unlike the order of successive events which remains static and
eternally set, events change or move through the dimensional form of
time.

Because of our goal-oriented activities, we continuously turn to new
events and activities, thereby making present anticipated states and
shoving the former series back into the past. Merleau-Ponty puts this
very clearly when he writes that protentions and retentions

> do not run from a central I, but from my perceptual field itself,
> so to speak, which draws along in its wake its own horizon of
> retentions, and bites into the future with its protentions. I do not
> pass through a series of instances of now, the images of which I
> preserve and which, placed end to end, make a line. With the
> arrival of every moment, its predecessor undergoes a change: I
> still have it in hand and it is still there, but already it is sinking
> away below the level of presents; in order to retain it, I need to
> reach through a thin layer of time. It is still the preceding
> moment, and I have the power to recapture it as it was just now;
> I am not cut off from it, but it would not belong to the past
> unless something had altered. It is beginning to be outlined
> against, or projected upon, my present, whereas it *was* my
> present a moment ago. When a third moment arrives, the second
> undergoes a new modification; from being a retention it becomes
> the retention of a retention, and the layer of time between it and
> me thickens.[23]

It is not that I sit around in a present through which events pass
from the future to the past. Of course, as we have already indicated, we

[21] Marcus Aurelius, *Meditations*, trans. G. M. A. Grube (Indianapolis, IN: Bobbs-Merrill,
1963) p. 34.
[22] See Aristotle, *Physics*, bk. I., chap. 10, 219b; Plotinus, *The Enneads*, trans. S.
Mackenna (London: Faber and Faber, 1962), pp. 229-33; and Kant, *Critique of Pure
Reason*, pp. 75-76.
[23] Merleau-Ponty, *Phenomenology of Perception*, pp. 416–17.

are consciously located in the present. But the future becomes the present by our acting to make it present. I do not observe the "flow" of temporal events, I perform it; I am not carried through time, I act it; I do not have time, I exist temporally. I am holding a gun ready to pull the trigger; I pull that trigger, let us say, and thereby make an anticipated "now" present and "fire" a former one into the past, retained and ready for recall.

> The upsurge of a fresh present does not *cause* a heaping up of the past and a tremor of the future; the fresh present *is* the passage of future to present, and of former present to past, and when time begins to move, it moves throughout its whole length.[24]

We propel ourselves forward toward anticipated goals by shoving the present and the whole past back into retention. It is not that we could ever suspend this turning to new "presents," thereby suspending the flow of time; such a suspension would be to do away with *ourselves*, as we will see later.

The flow of time, then, is closely connected with making present new activities. When it flows, it flows throughout the series. The distant future comes closer as I move toward it; and the past sinks back further and further until it recedes into obscurity.

Because in our activities we are oriented toward anticipated goals, time *seems* to flow from the future to the past; that is, the events in time pass by from the future to the past. Time seems to flow from the future to the past because *we* pass present actions toward the future. In other words, we make present anticipated actions and thus shove the present and the series of retentions into the past. As I dig into the future, I pass by acts and events which are pushed back into the retained past. Life is experienced as a flux, a "passingness" because *we* actively pass it by. Time is "moving" and "dying," a "perpetual perishing" and a "farewell," because it is the form and shape of our actions whereby we catapult ourselves from what has been to what is not yet.

[24] Merleau-Ponty, *Phenomenology of Perception*, p. 419.

Chapter Five

THE REFLECTIVE RELATION

> Presence to self . . . supposes that an impalpable fissure has slipped into being. If being is present to itself, it is because it is not wholly itself.
>
> —Sartre, *Being and Nothingness*

Consciousness and Experience

We shall mean by consciousness "awareness of objects."[1] "Through an act of consciousness, some object is presented to the experiencing subject and stands before the mind."[2] From this point of view, there is no such thing as consciousness without an object *of* which it is conscious. An essential element of consciousness therefore, is that it be *of* something or other, that it be presentational or "intentional" in character.[3] Every form of consciousness involves a presentational correlativity of a subject (dreamer, listener, lover) and a "meant" object (dream, tune, beloved) which is attended to and thus present to the conscious subject. It is a sort of *lumen naturale* by means of which a variety of kinds of objects become present to the conscious subject aware *of* them. It is the "clearing" in nature through which various forms of "what is" become present to consciousness and through which the modalities of the conscious subject ("me" seeing, hearing, etc.) likewise emerge over against those meant objects.

But this implies another important characteristic. Intentionality implies not only the correlative *relation* of a subject and an object; it also implies, of course, their *separation*. The subject of any act of consciousness is *not* the object, but is over against the object, and vice versa. A certain negation intrudes itself into the heart of the intentional and correlative act which consciousness is, a kind of radical otherness or "naught" at the heart of being. *In any act of consciousness a subject finds himself or herself present to an object of which he or she is conscious and from which he or she is "separated" by the intentional relation itself.*

These acts of consciousness, we should note carefully, take place in the larger continuity of experience, what James calls "the stream of

[1] John Dewey, *Experience and Nature* (New York: Dover Publications, 1958), p. 298.

[2] Aron Gurwitsch, *The Field of Consciousness* (Pittsburgh, PA: Duquesne University Press, 1964), pp. 3–4.

[3] Husserl, *Ideas*, p. 108.

thought."[4] I shall mean by "experience," here, just those sorts of temporal actions lived through by the agent involved which I discussed in the last chapter. The manifold of such experiences we can call the "life-world" or, as I prefer, "the world of ordinary experience."[5] This world is *not* a collection of object-entities, the "objective world." Rather, it is the horizon of our practical, bodily activity. We *live* this world, that is, we live the multiplicity of action-experiences which constitutes it. It is a "world," then, in which we directly act, relate, perceive, think, and make our way about. As Husserl put it, it is

> pregiven to us all quite naturally, as persons within the horizon of our fellow men, i.e., in every actual connection with others, as 'the' world common to us all. Thus it is . . . the constant ground of validity, an ever-available source of what is taken for granted, to which we, whether as practical men or as scientists, lay claim as a matter of course.[6]

We *are* this manifold of experiences, first of all. In other words, we directly and immediately live them through. Thus, we "run," "jump," "feel tired," and "go to the store" as well as "see the truck," "recall what we had for breakfast," "fear inflation," and "listen to the symphony." We "know our way about" this world of ordinary experience, as Wittgenstein put it, as a sort of "knowing how" rather than a knowing "that" or "what." I know how to run, for example, and I do not confuse that with telling time or remembering my first day in the army.

When I am running to catch the bus, I *am* that running, nothing but the bodily experience of wind, sweat, pumping lungs, aching muscles, and beating heart. And when I am seeing a blizzard, I am all seeing; I am this seeing subject conscious of the seen blizzard outside my window. While I am that "running" or "seeing" (or whatever experience), I am not thinking *about* them. I am not explicitly conscious of my "running" and "seeing," but only conscious of the bus I am running to catch or the blizzard.

> While we live so to speak in the act in question (when for example we lose ourselves in reading a story), then we do not notice anything of this I who is the center of reference of the accomplished acts.[7]

[4] William James, *Psychology, The Briefer Course*, ed. Gordon Allport (New York: Harper Torchbooks, 1961), p. 263.

[5] See P. Brockelman, *Existential Phenomenology and The World of Ordinary Experience: An Introduction* (Lanham, MD: University Press of America, 1980), pp. 55ff.

[6] Edmund Husserl, *Crisis of the European Sciences and Transcendental Phenomenology*, trans. D. Carr (Evanston, IL: Northwestern University Press, 1970), p. 122.

[7] Pierre Thevenaz, "Reflective Consciousness of Self," in *What is Phenomenology?*, ed. J. Edie (Chicago: Quadrangle, 1962), p. 117.

But this "world" or stream of experience has a very peculiar feature within it, namely that one kind of experience or conscious act we *can* perform within it is to become reflectively aware or self-conscious of the manifold of our concrete and prethematic experience, including consciousness itself. As Teilhard de Chardin has put it,

> reflection is, as the word indicates, the power acquired by a consciousness to turn in upon itself, to take possession of itself *as of an object* endowed with its own particular consistency and value: no longer merely to know, but to know oneself; no longer merely to know, but to know that one knows.[8]

When I do become conscious of the "me running for the bus" or "me seeing the blizzard," I am no longer simply the "running" or "seeing" experience, but a reflective consciousness *of* that experience: "What are you doing, Paul?" "I'm trying to catch that bus!"

It is true that I might still be running, but my experience (to me the agent) will no longer be *running* but a reflective consciousness *of* that running. Naturally, I could (and probably would, if I were going to catch that bus) switch my experience back to running for the bus. It is as if we knew that our running bodies have a sort of inertia on their own and that we could thus leave them for a moment to become conscious *of* them and then return to reunite our experience with that running a moment later.

The World of Ordinary Experience, Phenomenology, and Truth

Our immediate experience, at any rate, is *not* such a reflective consciousness of itself. On the other hand, though not explicitly and reflectively self conscious, those experiences *are* implicitly and prereflectively "aware" of themselves in a sort of *unthematized apperception*. In running for the bus, for example, though I am not explicitly conscious of it, I *am* implicitly aware of what I am doing. If I were not, then I would not be able to tell my friend what I was doing when he asked me. Indeed, to add to our definition, "experience" is nothing but these actions and modes of consciousness *prereflectively aware of themselves*. As Sartre has put it,

> every unreflected consciousness, being non-thetic consciousness of itself, leaves a non-thetic memory that one can consult.[9]

An implicit "awareness," then, attends any experiential behavior or mode of consciousness. While constituting one of the necessary conditions for

---

[8] Teilhard de Chardin, *The Phenomenon of Man* (New York: Harper Torchbooks, 1965), p. 165.

[9] Jean-Paul Sartre, *The Transcendence of the Ego*, trans. F. Williams and R. Kirkpatrick (New York: The Noonday Press, 1957), p. 46.

explicit and conscious reflection, it is, as I said, itself neither conscious nor reflective.

Such a prereflective awareness permits us to *distinguish* our experiences (I do not ordinarily confuse telling time and remembering my grandmother, for example). It is also *recuperative*. That is, it is the condition for the possibility of fully reflective awareness through which we can make our experiential "knowing how" into a "knowing that" by becoming reflectively conscious *of* it. It thereby becomes available for explicit verbal articulation or knowledge.[10] From this point of view, the world of ordinary experience is encountered as the implicit background against which I consciously reflect about it. That is why, for Merleau-Ponty, "the world is always already there before reflection begins as an inalienable presence."[11]

All acts of consciousness, I said earlier, are "intentional" in character, involve both a conscious subject and a meant object. That means that reflective consciousness—whereby through the act of recall we become conscious of the manifold of lived experience by consciously recalling it—is itself intentional. Experience becomes "object" to itself. And just as with any other intentional act of consciousness, in such reflective consciousness we find not only a correlative relation of subject and object, but also their separation. A separation slips into the midst of experience insofar as that reflective consciousness *of* experience is by that very fact *not the experience itself.* Reflective consciousness is a sort of relational distance at the heart of experience, a distance constituting a self-awareness of that experience, but a distance nevertheless.

This relationship between experience and a reflective consciousness *of* it, between the ordinary world of our temporal activities and the reflective power we have to focus upon and thematize it, is the basis of my entire analysis here. Put another way, the fact that we are not just a "temporal relation," but also within it a "reflective relation" *to* it, opens up the possibility of phenomenological description and understanding, including of course such an understanding of "self." Since this is so fundamental to what I have said so far and to what I intend to say in what follows, it might be helpful to pause just a moment to explore what I mean by such phenomenological understanding and truth.

As is no doubt perfectly evident by now, phenomenology is not interested in the objects of experience but experience itself; not the objects of perceiving, remembering, or imagining, but perceiving, remembering and imagining as such.

---

[10] Fraser Cowley, *Critique of British Empiricism* (New York: St. Martin's Press, 1968), p. 19.
[11] Merleau-Ponty, *Phenomenology of Perception*, p. vii.

> Phenomenology is reflexive description and analysis. It is not description and analysis of any objective aspect of the world, but of our experience of the world.[12]

And with respect to those experiences, the object of phenomenology is to make verbally *explicit* what until then is merely *implicit* to living through those experiences. It is the attempt to evoke, articulate, and generally make thematic, reflective, and conscious that which is until then merely pre-thematic, pre-reflective, and pre-conscious. We can only philosophically reflect upon and articulate that mute world which we pre-reflexively live and act. Our everyday experience, I am saying, is always broader and deeper than our words *about* it. That means that we will always have to struggle to say *more* about life since what we say *about* it is never the same as the *living* of it. But more importantly, it means that we have nowhere else to turn for philosophical analysis and exploration than our ordinary lives, that manifold of everyday activity in the world as we live it through. Our temporal actions, I am claiming, are *already* in the living, pregnant with an entire philosophy, if we only had the talent and discipline to focus upon it and conceptually set it out for view. As Paul Ricoeur has put it, "Phenomenology wagers that the lived can be understood and said."[13] That means we must turn our philosophical eyes back to our everyday and concrete experience *as we live it through.*

I think the implications of this for the *writing* of this sort of philosophy are beautifully and succinctly expressed by Michael Novak.

> Life is fuller than words. Words are poor and clumsy tools, though each of them is precious. Those who write constantly struggle to put black marks on a page, trying to signal a meaning to distant readers. Sometimes, the marks seem woefully inadequate. Often, in trying to express the experiences and meanings most important to us we keenly feel the limitations of our skills. The determination to get meanings into words—and to get them exactly—is thoroughly demanding. One key to its practice is to keep one's eye on the actual living of life, and not merely on other sets of words.[14]

What does this imply about "truth"? It certainly is the case that such early, so-called "pure" phenomenologists as Edmund Husserl seemed to have a rather "realistic" picture of knowledge and truth in mind. That is, they seemed to assume that if we could but "bracket" or set aside our distorting *assumptions* about experience long enough really to turn back to and reflectively "see" the essence (*Wesen*) of any particular "experience" ("the immanent object of perception"), then indeed it would simply be a

[12] F. Cowley, *Critique of British Empiricism*, p. 19.

[13] Paul Ricoeur, "Philosophy of Will and Action," *Phenomenology of Will and Action*, ed. Straus and Griffith (Pittsburgh, PA: Duquesne University Press, 1967), p. 17.

[14] Michael Novak, *Ascent of the Mountain, Flight of the Dove* (New York: Harper & Row, 1978), p. 213.

matter of choosing the most felicitous phrasing to express and communicate "it." Thus, in a certain way, any phenomenon is assumed to have a sort of static essence which just is and which can be grasped and communicated once we get beyond the build up of distortions and assumptions *about* it which we carry around with us. Naturally, the job of the phenomenologist from this point of view is to get "back to the things themselves" ("zu den Sachen selbst"), to clear away the distortions and get through to actual experience long enough to "see" it and "show" it just as it manifests itself. This is a sort of realism, for it is assumed that we *can* get back to actual experience and linguistically set it out for view just as it is, without any distorting additions from the mind or subject. Truth, then, becomes a *correspondence* between the declaratory proposition which describes the experience and the reality it is about.

The trouble with this view is that it overlooks some important aspects of language which have led such "existential" phenomenologists as Martin Heidegger, Hans-Georg Gadamer, Paul Ricoeur, and others to alter radically their (and my) conception of phenomenological understanding and truth.[15]

First of all, to make a familiar observation, a word or sign is not identical to its meaning; a gulf separates words and phrases from their various meanings. A word, for example, can have different meanings in different usage/contexts (it is polysemic), and the same meaning can be expressed by different words. "We . . . distinguish the word sound (or the written mark) from what it means as well as from what it denotes, names or refers to."[16]

But speaking is not just a random series of words with a variety of meanings familiarly associated with them according to situation and usage. On the contrary, language also displays rules of arrangement or syntax. Syntax can be defined as the a priori laws of composition of the word and phrase parts into meaningful whole sentences and paragraphs. We might say that syntax is what words need in order to be meaningful and communicative in their different ways; and words are what syntax needs in order to bring diversity of meaning to the a priori structure of language. Therefore, for a speaker to communicate meaning to another person there must be both universal rules of syntax as well as shared or "sedimented" meanings associated with words and phrases in their varying social and linguistic usages.

In speaking, as well as in a derivative sense in writing, we can say that a *speaker* speaks to *someone* about *something*. There is a kind of

---

15 Each of these philosophers is categorized in this manner simply to set them over against Husserl on this point.
16 James M. Edie, *Speaking and Meaning: The Phenomenology of Language* (Bloomington, IN: Indiana University Press, 1976), p. 131.

tripartite aspect to human discourse: person speaking, subject spoken about, and person spoken to. Using the a priori syntax, and sedimented or shared meanings associated with words in varying contexts, a speaker communicates meaning about something to someone. Normally we communicate merely sedimented meanings; we do not say anything new. But sometimes a speaker will disclose (say) new meaning about an old and familiar subject or reality. Furthermore, language historians are very familiar with the fact that new meanings actually emerge in the history of any particular language, and in their turn, become "familiar" and join the body of other sedimented meanings readily available to the users of that language. The question is: How do such new meanings develop? The formal syntax along with the body of shared meanings within any language simply cannot account for such novelty. Furthermore, the fact that words mean different things in different usage/contexts not only does not explain the phenomenon of novel meanings, but presupposes it. It would seem that language is *neither* a set of hard-and-fast rules along with a collection of dictionary meanings associated with various words and phrases in different contexts *nor* a hodgepodge of arbitrary and unique usages and novel meanings and no binding rules whatever. Clearly, it is *both*!

Let us recall the tripartite structure of discourse: a *speaker* who *speaks* about *something* to *someone*. By using syntax and sedimented meanings, a speaker intends to say something about something he is talking about. He struggles to stay in touch with the experience or reality he is talking about, and that intention animates his words and (as he struggles to say it) shifts the familiar meaning of the words *analogically*. Instead of simply utilizing a familiar and shared "dictionary" meaning, at creative moments we try to stick with the reality we are discussing, and we seek (intend) a meaning about it which has not yet been said. We struggle to express that novel meaning and do so by extending the meaning by analogy and metaphor. In other words, in such a circumstance, we say something new (a new meaning) about something to someone. If we say, "he wrapped himself in a mantle of sorrow," we have a metaphor in which the meaning of the words has been extended beyond their familiar sense to tell us something new about reality. In Ricoeur's terminology, there is within analogy and metaphor a "surplus of meaning" over the dictionary meaning.

> In a live metaphor the tension between the words, or, more precisely, between the two interpretations, one literal and the other metaphoric, at the level of the entire sentence elicits a veritable creation of meaning. . . . A metaphor is not an ornament of discourse. It has more than an emotive value because it offers new

information. A metaphor, in short, tells us something new about reality.[17]

Now, as we noted earlier, words and phrases are not identical to their (various) meanings. Rather, they are like windows through which we see various meanings depending on context and the intention of the speaker. "We see *through* expressions to what they express."[18] Through analogy and metaphor, a speaker extends meaning and thereby actually says something new about something to someone. The wondrous human ability to take something for something else seems to lie at the heart of this remarkable phenomenon. Sir Isaiah Berlin puts this magnificently in a recent article in *The Listener*.

> The only way in which you can explain things to people, usually, is by some kind of analogy, from the known to the unknown. You are faced with something puzzling: 'What is man?' 'What is human nature?' And you say: 'Well, human nature is rather like . . . zoology, botany—we know a good deal about that, human nature is not awfully unlike that.'[19]

As I hope is evident by now, this view of language has important implications for some wider philosophical issues and, in fact, for philosophy itself. Let us begin with the latter. If a gulf separates the word-expression from any meaning disclosed through it, then we are fated to an historical evolution and development of knowledge which will never be finished or fulfilled. That is, we will never achieve complete *Truth* because there is a separation *in principle* between an expression and *what* is expressed by it, in other words what the speaker is speaking about. All we have, and all we *can* have if this philosophical analysis of language be correct, are incomplete perspectives upon reality, illuminations of it, if you will, but never the epistemic *Eschaton* of completed Truth.

In fact, the same bifurcation between expression and meaning intended *through* it implies a conception of truth beyond the correspondence view. From this point of view, truth is closer to what Heidegger calls "apophansis," namely, *disclosure*.[20] The process of laying out the meaning or sense of any phenomenon is not, as it seemed to have been for Husserl, a simple matter of eidetic insight (*Wesenschau*) and then mere verbalization of that insight in words and sentences. Rather, from this point of view, truth or coming to understand phenomenologically

---

[17] Paul Ricoeur, *Interpretation Theory: Discourse and the Surplus of Meaning* (Fort Worth, TX: Texas Christian University, 1976), pp. 51, 52, 53.

[18] Edie, *Speaking and Meaning*, p. 159.

[19] Sir Isaiah Berlin, "Sir Isaiah Berlin on Men of Ideas and Children's Puzzles," *The Listener*, Jan. 26, 1978, p. 113.

[20] Heidegger, *Being and Time*, p. 261.

involves a complex series of steps. First of all, there must be a tearing away of the veil of "sedimented" meanings and opinions which gets in the way of an adequate encounter with the phenomenon in question. Secondly, a creative search (by analogy) for words and phrases to articulate the intended meaning of the phenomenon must follow. We do not "know" that meaning first and then simply clothe it in proper language. On the contrary, we come *truly* to know it in the very process of *disclosing-saying* it by means of the metaphorical extension of the meaning of the words and phrases involved. Struggling to *express* the meaning of a phenomenon is at the same time struggling to *disclose* or "know" it.

> When the poet says that 'nature is a temple where living columns . . . ,' the verb *to be* does not just connect the predicate *temple* to the subject *nature*. . . . The copula is not only relational. It implies besides, by means of the predicative relationship, that *what is* is redescribed: it says *that* things really are this way.[21]

And what is that "what is" or reality which we seek to express and see through our analogical and metaphorical extensions of meaning? *It is the manifold of our experience*, what we earlier called the world of ordinary experience. As we said, we directly live that "world" or the variety of experiences which constitute it. To understand it, we can and must develop a reflective distance from it. Then, in trying to evoke and say what that experience is like, we must struggle to verbally disclose it by means of analogy and metaphor—that is, by extending familiar meaning into a "disclosive" surplus of meaning more adequate to the reality we are trying to get at.

> Because we are in the world, because we are affected by situations, and because we orient ourselves comprehensively in those situations, we have something to say, we have experience to bring to language.[22]

So, we come full circle. A new phenomenological understanding of language has led to a fundamental revision of the notion of phenomenological truth and understanding from "correspondence" to "disclosure." That conception of truth as disclosure, of course, constitutes the foundation of the present study of time and self. Our ordinary experience is always more than one can say about it, and yet it is that experience, which lies behind what we say and which is the ideal *terminus ad quem*, which we seek in our descriptive disclosure.

---

[21] Paul Ricoeur, *The Rule of Metaphor*, trans. R. Czerny (Toronto: University of Toronto Press, 1977), pp. 247–48.

[22] Ricoeur, *Interpretation Theory*, pp. 20–21.

In more traditional terminology, "understanding" and "being" have always been associated together; for if understanding is not about "what is," then it cannot be "understanding" at all. It is "being" that we seek in our groping attempts to disclosively understand. "Being," here, means the excess of meaning within our ordinary experience over what has already been said or even could be said about it.

PART THREE:
SELF

Chapter Six

LIFE-VALUES AND THE NARRATIVE STRUCTURE
OF PERSONAL IDENTITY

Man is the only living thing that, in order to live, needs to give
himself reasons for existing. It is an extraordinary thing.

—Ortega y Gasset

Background

Several years ago I happened to hear the Canadian theologian, Gregory Baum, speak at the Episcopal Theological Seminary on the relevance
of the social sciences for contemporary theology. During his talk, Dr.
Baum referred to Freudian psychoanalytic theory as "mythological." Far
from a disparagement, he meant only to indicate (in spite of Freud's
own views) that at root the psychoanalytic model is not so much scientific and a way of understanding as it is a sort of interpretation or sense
of the significance of life. In that sense, it seems more like religious
vision and faith than science. Like all such interpretations of the significance of life, it appeals to us primarily in our periods of crisis and
despair, beckoning us to join in, to enter the psychoanalytic process and
discover a new sense of life which will make life deeper and better for
us. "Come," it seems to be saying, "join us and save yourself." The astonishing part of all of this is that in fact that does seem to be the case.
Those who do enter the process held out by the model of what human
life is all about actually *do* seem to change and deepen their lives fully
as much as those washed in the waters of the Jordan. However that may
be, psychoanalysis seems more like religious conversion than medical
remediation,[1] more a sense of what life is all about than a scientific
hypothesis, more an attitude *toward* life than a kind of science *about* it.

What struck me about all this was not simply viewing psychoanalysis
as a case of mythology; on the contrary, what really impressed me was
Baum's insight that mythology, in the sense of an interpretation of the
significance of life, lies at the *heart* of our personal identities and lives

---

[1] Perhaps this is not so astonishing, after all. Louis Dupré in his recent book points to
just such a "healing" and "liberating" aspect of traditional Christian soteriology. As he puts
it, "salvation itself is healing and . . . all actual healing is part of the redemptive process."
Louis Dupré, *Transcendent Selfhood* (New York: Seabury, 1976), p. 47.

rather than at their periphery as "bad science," "primitive explanation," or simply "lies" and "fantasy." As I said earlier in Chapter Two, there seems to be something extraordinary about being a "self"—something entirely outside science and cognitive understanding in general— namely, that a "self" is just the "self" it happens to be (what I shall call "personal identity") because of its *attitude* toward life.

A second event, which led to the reflections embodied in this chapter, was coming across an existential insight in the writings of both Karl Jaspers and Martin Heidegger. In the words of Jaspers, "the urge to being is an urge to selfhood."[2] The struggle to be more fully is precisely the struggle to determine one's personal identity, to discover or fill in who "I" am.

These two events, hearing Gregory Baum talk about psychoanalysis as mythological and reading Jasper's statement that the pursuit of being *is* the pursuit of identity, raised a number of philosophical background issues about the very nature of self which we ought to explore before advancing our own theory of self in the next chapter.

Attitudes Toward Life

As everyone knows, Kierkegaard and Nietzsche helped to initiate a rather remarkable revolution in the form and substance of contemporary philosophy and theology. Their views led to a new understanding of philosophy, an understanding with important implications for any philosophy of self. I mean this in a rather specific way. Their notions of "subjective truth" or "vital lies" have been at least one source for the hermeneutical insight that all explicit, systematic philosophies and theologies—far from being the bedrock upon which we might securely rest our Athens or Jerusalem—in actuality rest upon, presuppose, and (finally) mask a precognitive and personal sense of being or reality. This "subjective truth," what I would like to call here an "attitude toward life" or "life-value," is not a sort of conceptual hypothesis. Whatever truth or manner of verification it may involve certainly is not of the scientific or positivistic variety. Rather than being an intellectual and cognitive phenomenon, it is lived and behaved or acted through. It is a preconceptual, passionate, and personal vision or interpretation of what life and reality is about *for me*, a focal vision which does not precede my actions and behavior as much as it pervades them as their very sense.[3] Focusing on Kierkegaard for a moment, subjective truth is not a form of philosophy or metaphysics but something at the heart of "me"

---

[2] Karl Jaspers, *Philosophical Faith and Revelation* (New York: Harper & Row, 1967), p. 5.

[3] Søren Kierkegaard, *Concluding Unscientific Postscript*, trans. David Swenson (Princeton, NJ: Princeton University Press, 1944), pp. 182ff.

and my life, a meaningful doing rather than a kind of conceptual know-ing. As Kierkegaard put it in his *Journals*:

> What I really lack is to be clear about *what I am to do*, not what I am to know. . . . What good would it do me to be able to explain the meaning of Christianity if it had *no* deeper signifi-cance *for me and for my life*?[4]

An attitude toward life, then, is a personal preconceptual disclosure of the meaning of existence which precedes and prefigures any explicit philosophy or theology. In other words, any explicit philosophical articu-lation or "game" is preceded by an attitude or sense of how to play the game, the rules of the game to follow. In our sort of terminology, some-one must actively *care* about the game in order actually to start to play it or, indeed, to know what game he is playing. A life-value is not a philosophy or hypothesis. It is an attitude or sense of what matters and counts in life such that someone would existentially and actively care enough about it actually to do it. Without such a sense of what it means to be, no philosophy would ever have come into being. It is for this rea-son, it seems to me, that Heidegger tells us in *Being and Time* that "even the phenomenological 'intuition of essences' is grounded in exis-tential understanding."[5] Conceptual understanding, we are saying, rests upon and presupposes "existential understanding" or life-value; objective truth and science rest upon and presuppose a human attitude toward life.[6]

Remarkably enough, Kierkegaard and Nietzsche pulled the rug out from under the long tradition of rationalism by showing that it presup-poses real persons to whom such a life-pursuit *means* something. "Faith" (a synonym for "subjective truth" for Kierkegaard) is not "ignorance," "belief," or "pseudo-explanation"; Kierkegaard puts it back at the heart of life, so that philosophy and science presuppose and rest upon it.

We must keep in mind one caution here. We are not talking about a life-value or attitude toward life as some sort of consciousness locked-up in the body and separated from the world, a mind or subject which invents itself in the recesses of itself apart from and before bodily activ-ity. Rather, we are talking about active agents in the world of ordinary experience. *Life-values emerge through our everyday, concrete, tempo-ral activity*; in fact, they "inhabit" that activity as its raison d'être.

---

[4] Søren Kierkegaard, *Journals*, trans. Alexander Dru (London: Oxford University Press, 1938), p. 15; also, on "faith" as subjective truth, see Kierkegaard, *Postscript*, p. 182, where he identifies the two.

[5] Heidegger, *Being and Time*, p. 187.

[6] This does not mean, of course, that there can be no rational criticism of such attitudes toward life, nor that every life-value—simply because someone holds it—is as justified and valid as any other.

Action, as we have seen, is "intentional"; it is a temporal process whereby we actively reach out toward and achieve meaningful goals. In acting, we go beyond what "has been" and "is" toward intended or anticipated goals which "are not yet" but which become present when, in fact, we achieve them.

I was writing at my desk after breakfast when I heard the telephone ring downstairs. So, I got up from my desk, walked downstairs, picked up the phone, and said, "Hello." The action of answering the telephone is typical of such bodily, temporal activity. It takes place in the context of what I *was* doing (I had just had breakfast before writing at my desk), and the activity is an implicit and prereflexive (I do not think about it) doing and reaching out toward an intended goal (going downstairs to pick up the phone). When I achieved that anticipated goal, what was formerly future and merely intended becomes present, what was formerly present is shoved into the past, and what was past is pushed further into the past. That former present, as we saw, becomes the "already has been" which lies immediately behind the new present and which, along with the newly anticipated future, situates and constitutes the present action. Action is not *in* time nearly as much as it is a *temporal process* through which we transcend what is and has been toward what is possible. An attitude toward life is not something before or beside such temporal action but lies at the heart of it. Perhaps the best way to get at this is to take a brief look at what Heidegger in *Being and Time* calls "understanding," for that "understanding" is Heidegger's term for what we are calling an "attitude" or "life-value" and what Kierkegaard calls "subjective truth" or "faith."

"Understanding" for Heidegger is, first of all, an "existentiale."[7] That means, simply, that it is a necessary and universal structure of the world of ordinary experience. It is, he tells us, a "significance" or "for-the-sake-of-which" our actions and everyday work in that world intend or aim toward. Thus, we actively use various natural and artificial things around us as tools (things "ready-to-hand") in order to achieve this or that goal. I am right now sitting on a chair at my desk with books all around me and a coffee cup immediately to my right. I am typing and trying to finish this section of this essay in order—hopefully—to comprehend more clearly the relationship of "understanding" or life-value and personal identity. All those things around me are used instrumentally as tools to achieve what, for some unknown reason, is right now a meaningful goal of my activity, i.e., what I am trying to *do* here. Whatever doings in which I or we might be engaged contain an implicit "understanding" of

---

[7] Heidegger, *Being and Time*, pp. 182ff. Also, see Martin Heidegger, *The Basic Problems of Phenomenology*, trans. Albert Hofstadter (Bloomington, IN: Indiana University Press, 1982), pp. 275 and 279.

what the action intends or is all about—in the case above to finish part of this essay. Our knowing "about" books and typewriters and coffee cups, in the sense of knowing "how" to use them, depends on this active and intentional "understanding" or "for-the-sake-of-which" we use them.

"Understanding" is prereflexive and active, a caring for this or that meaningful goal which at the same time places all the entities we "understand" and "know about" into a meaning-context, thereby constituting a familiar "world" which we inhabit. It is a significance which moves and motivates us to act, the very sense of what the action is "for." I do not have to think about what I am doing, and usually I do not unless my action is thwarted or I am asked about it.

"What are you doing?" someone might say to me.

"Oh, I'm working on my essay on time and personal identity which I have to have finished by . . ."

"Understanding" for Heidegger is *not* conceptual knowledge, but the existential basis for it. "Understanding is not a mode of cognition, but the basic determination of existing."[8] It is a kind of "knowing one's way about" which goes along with and structures our ordinary goal-directed behavior, a way of "seeing" life "as" this or that.[9] It is, then, a preconceptual, lived "sight" or disclosure of "possible" being within action itself. The "caring" for such goals is such that we actively seek them; indeed, the seeking *is* the caring!

Finally, Heidegger tells us that "understanding" discloses the meaning or sense of being.

> In the way in which its Being is projected both upon the 'for-the-sake-of-which' and upon significance (the world), there lies the disclosedness of Being in general.[10]

There is about our temporal activity and experience an anticipated, future "not yet" which we are seeking actively to bring into being. We encounter being in our own temporal, incomplete, and open-ended striving or seeking *to be*. Or, as Heidegger puts the same thing, "Being has to do with an origin that always comes to meet us from the future."[11]

---

[8] Heidegger, *The Basic Problems*, p. 278.

[9] An interesting comparison might be drawn here between Heidegger's notion of "understanding" as "sight" and Wittgenstein's analysis of "seeing-as" or "seeing aspects" in the *Philosophical Investigations*. For an interesting discussion of this, see David B. Seligman, "Wittgenstein on Seeing Aspects and Experiencing Meanings," *Philosophy and Phenomenological Research* 37 (1976): 205–17. Also, for some of the theological parallels and implications of this direction, see John Wisdom, "Gods," in *Classical and Contemporary Readings in Philosophy of Religion*, ed. John Hick (Englewood Cliffs, NJ: Prentice-Hall, 1970), pp. 429–45; and John Hick, *God and the Universe of Faith* (London: Macmillan, 1973), chap. 3.

[10] Heidegger, *Being and Time*, p. 187.

[11] Martin Heidegger, *On the Way to Language*, trans. Peter Hertz (New York: Harper & Row, 1971), p. 10. Also, see Heidegger, *The Basic Problems*, pp. 298ff.

In our goal-directed activity, we seek to bring some significant future into actual existence, to become it or make it *be*. Understanding is nothing but this active, preconceptual striving for "possible" being. As Heidegger puts it, "Dasein is occupied in its own being with its ability to be."[12] This ultimate "for-the-sake-of-which" is an interpretation by somebody of what it means to be. Our activity itself embodies and releases an ultimate and overarching sense of what existence is all about, what is significant for us, what we care about. *The way we exist, what we do, discloses what matters for us, what we think is fundamental and most "real," "basic," or "focal" in living.* Kant's notorious punctuality in his daily strolls through Koenigsberg, we might imagine, was a kind of doing which in fact loudly announced to his fellow citizens something about Kant and his sense of what his life as a scholar and philosopher was all about. An attitude toward life is the sense of existence embodied in a person's temporal activity, the significance which his actions in general are ultimately "for" and which they seek to achieve.

"How do we develop life-values?" you might ask. "How are they formed?" Our immediate response ought to be, "Not easily." Each of us knows from his or her own periods of life-crisis that reorienting and redirecting life and self is no simple task. Experientially, life-values seem to be neither "invented" by the subject nor merely "uncovered" or "stumbled upon." We all know the process is far more difficult than that. In order to help us focus on the experience involved, let us take a brief look at what I think is a rather typical example.

> It was five years ago that my former husband left me and our two kids after ten years of marriage. One day, he just walked out and never came back. Of course, it was not totally a surprise. Things had been getting worse and worse for several years. I seemed always to be yelling at him and he just withdrew into his job and himself. We seemed to be from very different worlds.
>
> Anyway, I was both terrified and devastated. What was I supposed to do with two kids? How could we survive? I was really afraid. I had never learned any skills to support myself and the children. Bob and I got married right after high school and I thought the real purpose of life for a woman was to love her husband, make a warm home, and raise a family. That's the way it had always been in my family.
>
> I felt a mixture of fear for the future and self-incrimination. After all, everyone knows that it's the woman's job to keep her man 'happy.' Clearly, I had failed.
>
> Everyone was very kind to me at first. I learned from my friends that I was not the first woman to go through this. With some help

12 Heidegger, *The Basic Problems*, p. 295.

from my family and AFDC, we managed to just barely scrape by.

But that wasn't the hardest part of that first year. I was both angry and down on myself. I was angry at my husband and 'life' for doing this to me. At the same time, I felt more and more depressed. I felt trapped and worthless, as if my life (I mean 'me') was going nowhere. I couldn't connect to the world around me in any meaningful way. As I said, my so-called 'marketable skills' were just about zero. As my depression set in, I found it increasingly difficult even to go out on a job interview, because that only increased my feeling of failure. I felt like I had no future. I was depressed, afraid, trapped, disintegrating in anxiety.

I spent most of my time watching TV and drinking a lot, a whole lot. I felt I was in suspended animation, as if I had stopped living. The drinking actually helped, at least while I was drinking. What I mean is that while I was drinking I felt everything was *possible*. Who knows . . . maybe I would get 'discovered' and become a famous model or TV star. Dreams! Phantom images of the possible in a life bereft of possibility. Yes, dreams! But as long as they lasted, they pushed back the hopelessness.

Finally, some girlfriends of mine convinced me to join a therapy group down at the church. Me? Yes. It was hard, but I did it. In fact, I felt like I had no choice. It was either that or I would go crazy!

I won't bore you with all the details. It was hard, really hard for me. I had to let go of my old images of what it means to be a woman and mother; I had to let go of myself, everything I had been. But more importantly, I had to find out who I was or wanted to be. That was the hardest part, because I didn't know. It wasn't as if I could sit there with the group and either *discover* the 'real' 'me' who had always existed underneath the debris of her shattered life or *invent* some 'me' and then go out and become it. Oh no. There was no 'me' to discover and if I had known what 'me' to invent, I wouldn't be there!

What I had to do was to explore and try out various possibilities. With the support of the group, I went back to school (it absolutely terrified me at first) in an Associates Degree program at Stratford Community College. I didn't know what courses to take or what program to get into. I tried Secretarial—I hated it. I tried Bookkeeping—ditto. It took several years of therapy, courses and various programs before I tried a nursing course. I seemed to do pretty well, and the teacher encouraged me. I took some more courses and finally joined the nursing program.

Anyway, to make a long story short, I'm now a nurse practitioner. I work twenty hours a week at Cardinal Fuentes Hospital. I like it and I actually get paid. I just enrolled in the full nursing program. I'm going to become a registered nurse. Me! Can you imagine that?

Obviously, such a period of reorientation to new life-values entails a difficult process of alienation, exploration, and discovery. First of all, we should note that the disintegration of self entails at the same time a temporal disintegration; in this case no sense of an anticipated, "possible" future and a distancing from the painful past and present. It is as if one were living day-to-day in a tedious, fragmented time, coming from nowhere and going nowhere. Secondly, and more positively, it involves becoming aware of earlier life-values in order to let them go, or at least to integrate them in new ones. This is quite clearly a painful experience insofar as it means (as we shall see) going beyond "who" one has been. But the process does not end there. Because action is necessarily temporal, one must then "find" or "develop" *new* life-values or meaningful goals of life toward which to work. As we said earlier, such new life-values are neither made up by the subject nor simply stumbled upon, but emerge as possibilities in a sort of active and intimate dialogue with life. The process is a sometimes painful, sometimes joyful, but always difficult letting-go and letting-be, listening, unfolding discovery of significant possibilities and goals toward which "I" can act and come to be.

The Narrative Structure of Personal Identity

As we saw earlier, temporality is the very form or structure of our active doings.

> I was on the way to the library from my apartment. I wanted to look up a book so that I could finish writing my essay on witchcraft in sixteenth-century Provence. I was over by Sheridan, right near the Deli, when suddenly just as I stepped off the curbing, I was hit by a car which swerved around the corner. All I saw was a blur, then a flash of light in my head. The next thing I knew was in the hospital and my wife was whispering, 'It's okay, Paul, you're going to be okay.'

The temporal actions, here, are not independent and discrete moments unconnected to one another like separate ticks of a clock. In stepping off the curbing, I was acting toward the anticipated goal of getting to the library in order to look up a book. That stepping off the curbing followed just *after* walking from my apartment along the sidewalk to that part of Sheridan near the Deli. The point I am trying to make is that our actions contain what I have called earlier "co-referentiality," a reference within any temporal action to what *has just been* and a reference out ahead to what the action intends or *anticipates*. Every action is situated and only makes sense within the horizon of past actions that lead to it and intended goals that it reaches toward. Notice, also, that the horizon of pastness or "just-having-been-ness" which helps to situate any action is replete with its own intentionality which points ahead and is fulfilled now or later. My stepping off the curbing on Sheridan is an action which coreferentially refers back to my having just walked up to Sheridan from my apartment and ahead to crossing the street so that I could get to the library to take out that book. The action is temporally situated because it is pregnant with coreferential or thetic ties to earlier and later actions.

We have argued that attitudes toward life emerge within these temporal activities as their ultimate "for-the-sake-of-which." An attitude toward life is a preconceptual understanding of what matters to us in life which we *actively* aim our lives toward and restlessly seek to bring about. It is a significance or sense of what is important and valuable such that we care enough about it actually to bring it into being. "To understand," as Heidegger puts it, "means . . . to project oneself upon a possibility."[13] What this means, of course, is that such attitudes toward life are constitutive of *ourselves*.

In what follows, we shall mean by "personal identity" the particular, individual "self" which each of us is or comes to be: it is "who" each of us is. We will not mean by "personal identity" *selfness* or the universal, human structure of *selfhood*, i. e., the evident fact that being some sort of self is part and parcel of being human. The former might be considered to be the existential, actual, or ontic embodiment of the latter; and the latter—selfness or the human structure of self which we will discuss in Chapter Seven—can be thought of as the ontological condition for the possibility of the former.

What does my active reaching out toward what I take to be fundamental and meaningful about living contribute to my personal identity or "me"? It contributes: (1) a sense of *transcendence*; (2) the phenomenon of *agency*; (3) the *substance* of who "I" am or what "I" am all about; and (4) a *narrativity* which structures and is essential to "me" and my life.

1. Transcendence

Being out ahead of myself in my active understanding means that "I" am *more* than what "I" have been and am now. A certain element of transcendence slips into existence, a transcendence or moreness that is an essential characteristic of personal identity. "I" am among other things sheer *openness* or *unfinishedness* because "I" actively seek to be *more*. We do not mean by this that "I" am a self-contained ego which then projects itself ahead of itself. That is the kind of category mistake we referred to earlier which thinks of personal identity as a sort of self-contained "thing" or entity. On the contrary, personal identity *includes*

---

[13] Heidegger, *The Basic Problems*, p. 277.

transcendence. *Possible being is part of the very reality of "me."*

> Dasein is as such out beyond itself. Only a being to whose onto-
> logical constitution transcendence belongs has the possibility of
> being anything like a self.[14]

2. Agency

Actively being out ahead of myself in my understanding brings to
"me" and my life a sense of *agency* because it entails *bringing* what is
only "possible" into actuality. By reaching out toward goals which are
understood to be crucial to living, "I" manifest a remarkable ability to
bring something about, and that power or ability is part of "me."
"Dasein is occupied in its own being with its ability to be."[15] "Being
able" is a defining characteristic of personal identity.

3. Substance

Attitudes toward life are part of the *substance* of personal identity.
Reaching toward what "I" find fundamental and meaningful about life
at the same time constitutes an affective unfolding of who "I" will be or
become. Let us say that "I" want to ameliorate the condition of the poor
and deprived and that "I" think the best way to do that is to become a
civil rights lawyer. "I" go to law school and *become* that. Or take the
extraordinary example of the Russian writer Aleksandr Solzhenitsyn. He
tells us that he was so appalled by the monstrous and arbitrary world of
Soviet prison camps in which he found himself that he feared it would
remain hidden and eternally unknown to the rest of the world. This was
such a painful possibility for him that he dedicated his life to the goal of
writing and making that history public, carefully remembering it in all
its daily detail and misery. He aimed his life at keeping the memory
alive, so that it could not happen again and as a sort of testimonial to the
victims. This is (at least in part) "who" Solzhenitsyn is, the substance and
vision at the heart of his life and person. We can almost see this remarkable vision and attitude toward life emerge in *The First Circle.* Two
prisoners have risen early to saw wood for the kitchen. They do this
work voluntarily, on top of their daily labors, but only under the stipula-
tion that no guard be present. One of the prisoners is Sologdin, aged 38;
the other is Nerzhin, 31. Sologdin has offered to teach Nerzhin

---

[14] Heidegger, *The Basic Problems*, p. 300. It would be interesting to try to trace the
origin of the notion of "soul" back to this aspect of ourselves. It would be all the more
interesting (as Heidegger might say) insofar as the conception of soul got reified into a
soul "substance" or "*res cogitans*" by a tradition which which has willy-nilly reduced
Being to "entities" or "things" present to us.

[15] Heidegger, *The Basic Problems*, p. 295.

". . . some of my rules . . . [on] how to face difficulties." Sologdin speaks:

> 'In the realm of the unknown, difficulties must be viewed as *hidden treasure!* Usually, the more difficult, the better. It's not as valuable if your difficulties stem from your own inner struggle. But when difficulties arise out of increasing objective resistance, that's *marvelous!*'

> The rosy dawn now shone on the flushed face of Aleksandr Nevsky [Sologdin], as if conveying the radiance of difficulties wonderful as the sun.

> 'The most rewarding path of investigation is: "the greatest external resistance in the presence of the least internal resistance." Failures must be considered the cue for further application of effort and concentration of will power. And if substantial efforts have already been made, the failures are all the more joyous. It means that our crowbar has struck the iron box containing the treasure. Overcoming the increased difficulties is all the more valuable because in failure the *growth of the person performing the task* takes place in proportion to the difficulty encountered!'[16]

To know "me" it is not enough to know my past and present. You must also know my hopes and dreams, who "I" want to become. In Solzhenitsyn's case, "to be" means to be hard and to endure in order to tell the story of the prison camps.

> Understanding as Dasein's self-projection is Dasein's fundamental mode of *happening*. As we may also say, it is the authentic meaning of action.[17]

Jaspers was right! "The urge to being is an urge to selfhood."

4. Narrativity

It is important at this point to recognize that we are not holding the view that personal identity is an unchanging and transcendental ego which simply happens to project itself into the future. Neither are we holding (with Sartre) the contrary view that personal identity is sheer existentiality, i.e., invents itself anew at each moment by negating what it has been in favor of a dream it seeks to become. No. Because of the coreferential structure of our temporal activity, personal identity is both a continuity with its past and a breaking with that past by actively seeking to be more. It is neither the one nor the other exclusively, but both. If we are free, it is a freedom which is situated and constrained by the particular past and present in which we find ourselves engaged.

---

[16] Aleksandr Solzhenitsyn, *The First Circle*, trans. T. P. Whitney (New York: Bantam Books, 1969), pp. 160–61.
[17] Heidegger, *The Basic Problems*, p. 277.

Of course, neither life-values nor the personal identity constituted by them take place outside the flow of time. In fact, as I have been arguing, they are actually part of that active, temporal process. That means, so to speak, that personal identity gets "stretched" over time. "I" am not merely the past, present, or future that "I" anticipate—*but all three.* There is a sort of temporal "thickness" to personal identity. To understand "me," you must understand where "I" have come from, my present situation and involvements, and where "I" am headed in my life.

Furthermore, this temporal extendedness or thickness of personal identity means that "I" am neither simply a sheer continuity (a same and single "me" over time) nor simply fragmented into a series of different "me"s, but both. Because each temporal action is solid with coreferential ties to the past and future and can be recalled as such, there is about the flow of my temporal experience a continuity which is "me." At the same time, however, that overarching personal identity binds together a series of discontinuous and different "me"s, e.g., "me" at twelve, twenty, twenty-five, and thirty years of age. The series of different personal identities are strung together and yet maintain their differences by the attitude toward life which I am presently actively seeking to bring about.

In this sense, our lives are a kind of *narrative* or emerging personal story, and in fact are recalled that way.

> The human being alone among the creatures on the earth is a storytelling animal: sees the present rising out of a past, heading into a future; perceives reality in narrative form.[18]

Like any narrative, there is a syntax or order in which each event of a person's life takes its place, is given its peculiar meaning, and is interrelated with the other events and the whole by the overarching narrative meaning or telos toward which the story is unfolding. As Claude Bremond puts it while discussing narrative form in general,

> An action can only be recognized as filling some function when account is taken of its place in the narrative process. . . . The organic solidarity of the whole directs the order of succession of the parts.[19]

Paul Ricoeur makes the same point when he says, "The Plot's configuration superimposes 'the sense of ending'—to use Kermode's expression—on the open-endedness of mere succession."[20]

---

[18] Michael Novak, "Story and Experience," *Religion As Story*, ed. James B. Wiggins (New York: Harper & Row, 1975), p. 175.

[19] Claude Bremond, "The Narrative Message," *Semeia* 10 (1978): p. 10; also, see Paul Ricoeur, "The Human Experience of Time and Narrative," *Research in Phenomenology* 9 (1979): pp. 24, 27.

[20] Ricoeur, "The Human Experience of Time and Narrative," p. 28.

Our lives contain both episodic events and a meaningful configuration or continuity which pulls them together into the particular story involved. That meaningful configuration in which the separate events and phases of our lives find their places within the evolving story is supplied by the life-value we are presently intending "here" at the "end" of the story. If a story is a narrative of events arranged in a temporal sequence, then "plot" is a narrative which involves an intended sense of what matters in life, an attitude toward life which "shows how it all hangs together and makes sense."[21] Our lives and selves are structured as a narrative plot, a plot which reveals *why* the events of the person's story are as they are by disclosing what they are *for*.

> Jung says we must look at the intentionality of the characters and where they are heading, for they are the main influence upon the shape of the stories. Each carries his own plot with him, writing his story, both backwards and forwards, as he individuates.[22]

Without life-values and the temporal action of which they are part, personal identity could not and would not be narratively structured; with such life-values, it necessarily is.

Our claim is a simple and straightforward one: life-values, temporally embodied in our active lives as personal narratives or stories, constitute the form and substance of personal identity. As Kierkegaard put it, "choice itself is decisive for the content of personality."[23] The more choice, the stronger personal identity becomes. Kierkegaard, of course, means by "choice" subjective truth or what we have termed life-values. Thus, we can say with him, "who" I am is tied up with that narrative meaning which lies within my actions and binds them together into a single and meaningful plot or personal story. If you want to know "me" (indeed, if I want to "know" myself), you must learn my personal story. The personal story I tell you is precisely a verbalization of the thematic attitude toward life which threads through my everyday life and actions.

For example, if you want to get to know me, you might ask me to

---

[21] James Hillman, "The Fiction of Case History: A Round," *Religion As Story*, pp. 129–30.

[22] J. Hillman, "The Fiction of Case History," p. 131.

[23] Søren Kierkegaard, *Either/Or*, in Bretall, ed., *Kierkegaard Anthology* (New York: Modern Library, 1938), p. 102. For Kierkegaard, "I" am a temporal relation between "necessity" and "possibility," the past and the future, and joined together by "choice" in the present. But "I" am not just that primary relation; "I" am also a relation to that. If "I" become the primary temporal relation, "I" exist fully as a self. Thus, the more "choice," the more self. If "I" refuse to relate myself to the primary temporal relation or process which "I" am (i.e., refuse to "choose") then "I" exist in a shadowy sense, what he sometimes calls "despair" or "esthetic existence." This is in effect an attempt not to be a self. See Søren Kierkegaard, *The Sickness Unto Death*, trans. W. Lowrie (Princeton, NJ: Princeton University Press, 1968), pp. 146ff., 197.

tell you about myself. If I sense that you want to get to know me only superficially, or if I do not want to initiate intimacy, I probably would tell you some objective sorts of things about myself like what I do for a living, where I live, and so on. It is a way of "delivering" (I tell you something) and is socially acceptable, but it keeps things from going too far. But if that is not the case, if in fact I want you to get to know me more personally and deeply, then I begin to tell you my "personal story." Perhaps I cannot tell it all to you, perhaps I forget parts, perhaps I select out of it what I want you to know about me, but the telling of my "personal story" is communicating to another (and myself) *who* I am.

One of the first things that is interesting about all of this is the seeming phenomenological fact that even if I am a bad story teller, a personal story is essentially fascinating and "real" to other persons and myself. Indeed, if it is not, then it is not a personal story at all; it is artificial and "out of touch." I believe that this is so precisely because a personal story is narratively woven around a person's life-value, his or her sense of what really matters. That is what makes it "personal" and "real" and what makes getting to know a personal story getting to know a *person*, i.e., what his or her particular life (to that person) is all about.

If I am asked who I am, I think back in my life and I tell a story about the "ups" and "downs" and "interconnections" of my life, not in terms of a series of factual and objective events nor an objective chronicle of my life, but a story about the important, meaningful ups and downs of my life—my hopes and fears, my carings, my successes and failures, etc. For example, just to take a small piece of a personal story:

> I remember when I was thirteen. It was spring. I'd just gotten out of the hospital for what seemed to me the hundredth time. I had almost died, this time, and it seemed like I was in the hospital every year while my friends were out playing baseball. Anyway, I was out, it was May, and my mother was taking care of me. She was fattening me up with eggnogs, I remember—two a day. She set me out in the back yard of our house, in a wicker chair and with an old khaki army blanket wrapped around me to keep me warm. The sun warmed me right through the blanket. Tulips, daffodils, and jonquils were in bloom and the grass was new and light green. I sat there the whole day. Although I had no words to describe or categorize it—nor did I want to—I felt like I was part of the garden. I felt one with the spring. I felt *myself* in bloom, fantastically alive, exuberant, deeply existing. It was so clear and so hard to talk about. Just *being* was what it was all about and that was plenty! I sat there all day.

> After that, I got better and I went back to school. In one way, I forgot about that garden experience, or at least I got involved in other things. Yet, in another way, I didn't forget it, for after that I always compared the depth and reality of my life to that 'day.' It became a kind of benchmark for me, a standard which I used

to measure how fully I was living. Later, I renewed the experience in different ways and circumstances. But it was only when I was in college that I learned that others had such experiences, and that they called them 'religious' or 'mystical.'

Of course, this is only one little segment of the larger story which constitutes a person's life. We could go on with the story. But notice, even with such a brief example, the story is bound together in terms of what is *now* seen as the fundamental sense or thread of it all. The various actions lead up to and away from what in the story is remembered as a particularly focal and significant action, the experience of oneness with the garden. Our personal stories are narrated in terms of a meaning-thread which holds them together. Success, failure, others, catastrophes, fears, hatreds, loves—all these take their place within the narrative thread of significance which strings the actions of our lives together. The story is not flat and one dimensional, then, but has its "ups" and "downs" in terms of the vision of what it is all about which holds it together.

Whether I am telling you only a part or the whole of my personal story, that telling discloses to you *who* I am. It tells you about the vision of life and personal character at the heart of my actions. It is an authentic personal story insofar as it reveals, along with the series of actions which make up my life, the life-value or sense of reality which informs those actions and which makes those actions *mine*, more than just a series of unrelated and discrete events. You get to know me through my personal story, because that personal story is personal, a story of my life which contains within it a sense of what matters. "Ah," you might say, "he is that mystical person who seems focused on experiencing wonder and awe in the face of the remarkable fact *that* he is at all. He seems fixed on 'isness.'" "When we tell our tales, we give away our souls," as James Hillman has put it.[24]

Lastly, note that if a person should change his or her attitude toward life, if he should become "converted" (to use religious terminology) to a new sense of things, then of course his personal story will also change. He will *see* his past actions differently, with different "ups" and "downs," and with a different thread of meaning connecting the narrative. Indeed, what he had earlier remembered, he might actually forget, and vice versa. It will be a different story because it will have a different vision or sense of existence about it now. The former attitude, however, will be remembered and will take its place as part of the new vision and

---

[24] James Hillman, *The Myth of Analysis: Three Essays in Archetypal Psychology* (Evanston, IL: Northwestern University Press, 1972), p. 182. This is what the psychologist, George Kelly, means by a "construct," i.e., a category of meaning by means of which we construe ourselves and the world. See George Kelly, *The Psychology of Personal Constructs* (New York: Norton, 1955).

new personal story. We might imagine, for example, that the author of
the above "mystical" story of the garden experience has grown up and in
the meantime become a social revolutionary. Then a new sense of life
has emerged, a sense of radical historicality and the need to will and
actively transform the human condition in order to alter the future and
overcome suffering. After such a "conversion," in looking back to the
earlier garden incident, he might say:

> What a down period of my life that was. I had been sick every
> year for five years. I guess I was just happy to be alive. But, you
> know, I think the whole thing was a very depressed and depres-
> sing time of my life. I was so down that I had to dream of reli-
> gious experiences when in fact all I really needed and wanted
> was to get hold of my life, to feel in control, to cease this feeling
> of things happening *to* me. Instead of doing that, I fantasized
> about mystical experiences and God. Anyway, I got over that
> later in college. I began to see how and why people—in fact
> whole classes—can be so alienated from living that they have to
> fantasize such living. As I gradually took more and more control
> of my life, I found such fantasy less and less necessary.

So, the meaning-thread at the center of the actions and narrative has
changed, and the whole is now seen from or through that new life-value
and vision. With such a conversion, life takes on a new or at least modi-
fied sense of what counts, and the past is seen from that new perspective.
But the earlier attitude, as well as the identity that went with it, is not
simply forgotten; it takes its place within the new one.

Finally, of course, the change in what one cares about means not
only a new personal story, but by that very fact, a new or changed personal identity.

> I was a mystic back in those depressed and romantic days, but
> now I'm working hard for the revolution. We don't need *that*
> nonsense any more. Mystics dream the world; we change it!

If it is true that "who-I-am-in-the-world is the gigantic assumption upon
which I rely in order for my experience to be meaningful at all to
me,"[25] it is likewise the case that "who" I am is intimately tied up with
the attitude toward life which underlies my personal story and threads
through my actions to make them a narrative.

As you can see, an attitude toward life is so close to us that we often
overlook it. It is the meaning-content or total interpretive sense of what
matters within the temporal structure of action, that thread of significance which ties those actions together coreferentially and makes of
them a personal story or narrative.

---

[25] Ernest Keen, *Primer in Phenomenological Psychology* (New York: Rinehart and
Winston, 1975), p. 23.

When persons act, their actions 'tell a story.' That is, action always has implicit within it the agent's sense of who he is, where he is, what his situation is, how his action affects that situation, what direction his action is carrying him, etc. In a word, action implies a view of the world. The fundamental fact about action is the imagined story that gives it shape. A person who is acting out the story of 'the advance of science' discriminates accordingly what to do and what not to do, the manner of his acting, its satisfactions and disappointments, and its consequences. To participate in such a story is what is meant by being religious.[26]

---

[26] M. Novak, *Ascent of the Mountain*, pp. 132–33. It might be claimed that the wide variety of cultural forms of narrative (story, novel, opera, poem, drama, film, mythology, history, parable, sacred theology) are simply modes of discourse appropriate to that entity basically characterized by such temporal *narrativity*. Indeed, Paul Ricoeur has made just such a transcendental argument. See Ricoeur, "The Human Experience of Time and Narrative," pp. 17, 23, 24. For a similar argument, see Stephen Crites, "The Narrative Quality of Experience," *Journal of the American Academy of Religion*, 39 (1971): pp. 291–311.

Chapter Seven
TIME AND SELF

> Thus from its first arising, consciousness by the pure nihilating movement of reflection makes itself personal; for what confers personal existence on a being is not the possession of an Ego—which is only the sign of the personality—but it is the fact that the being exists for itself as a presence to itself.
>
> —Sartre, *Being and Nothingness*

A Look Back

In moving toward our phenomenological conception of self, it might be helpful to review briefly what we have so far argued in this book.

First of all, rather than seeing human life as a sort of passive observation and conceptualization of the "real world" out there, we have been sketching a picture of ordinary and everyday human action as fundamental and pivotal. We set out to get at that by phenomenologically laying out the nature of such action as we, the agents, experientially live it through. Thus, such experienced action is always "contextual" and "intentional," i.e., conditioned and yet aimed at a goal which it seeks to achieve.

That led us to what we called "temporality" or "the temporal relation," the very form of such mundane activity. Actions embody temporality insofar as they are doings which reach out of a retained context toward an anticipated goal. To act is to be temporal. And such temporal actions are preconscious or prereflective, simply lived through.

Each such doing or present action retains this horizon of contextuality and anticipation in a phenomenon which we called "coreferentiality." Each "now," each present doing, embodies referential ties to what has been and to what is anticipated in the doing itself. And because of that "coreferentiality," the series of "nows" can be recalled complete with a unity or continuity which binds them into both a single time and a serial difference, successively related as "before" and "after."

But our active experience embodies more than just this primary or "temporal relation." We are also capable of a secondary activity in the flow of experience, what we called "reflection" or the "reflective relation." By conscious "recall" or "expectation" of the retained or anticipated "nows," we can become explicitly conscious of the primary, preconscious but apperceived temporal relation or flow of everyday activities, including of course its "coreferential" structure.

Perhaps most importantly of all, our ordinary temporal activities exhibit a remarkable phenomenon that we called "attitudes toward life" or "life-values." Such life-values are a person's sense of what is fundamental about living, and they pervade and sleep within that person's actions as the very sense of what the actions are ultimately *for*. We actively reach out toward such "possible" life-values in order to bring them into being. Insofar as we do, we bring ourselves into being.

In other words, "personal identity" is defined by such active attitudes toward life. An "I" necessarily involves "possible being" or "openness;" a sense of "agency" or "being able;" and a "substance" or "content" which is gained from the temporal and active reaching out to actualize life-values. "Who I am is tied up with that narrative meaning which lies within my actions and binds them together into a single and meaningful plot or personal story."[1]

Being part of an active, temporal process, such life-values and the personal identity they entail are stretched over time and exhibit what we called a temporal "extendedness" or "thickness." "I" am neither the past, the present, nor the future *alone*, but all three.

We are fated to be temporal, through and through. What this means, finally, is that personal identity is *structured narratively*. "I" do not exist like an entity or thing locked up and entombed in a present "now." Rather, "I" am a temporally active agent existing narratively. I am a series of events which are strung together coreferentially into a meaningful narrative whole, coming from somewhere and going somewhere. "I" am an emerging story in the process of happening.

The Self Is A Double Relation

In the midst of our everyday lives, each of us (in a sense yet to be stipulated) is aware of himself or herself as a subject or self. It is this subjective relation to ourselves as active agents in the world that I want to explore. As I have already indicated, such subjectivity is never to itself a sort of objective entity or "thing." It is not a kind of entity which either remains "present" throughout the series of different temporal moments or gets shrunken into any particular, fragmented moment in the linear chain of such moments. It is not a "thing" to be bumped into and merely observed, like a mountain or a boulder. Rather, we want to claim with both Hegel and Kierkegaard that the self is a *relation*, or rather a *set* of relations.[2] Perhaps the best way to get at this phenomenon is to set out

---

[1] Chapter Six.

[2] Both Hegel and Kierkegaard claimed that the self is not so much a static substance as a dynamic process and set of relations. For example, see Mark C. Taylor, *Journeys to*

our definition of the self first and then try to unpack and articulate it. First, the definition: *The self is a temporal relation which reflectively relates itself to itself. It is not merely that temporal relation, then, but also a reflective relationship and attitude to that.*

First of all, "the self is a temporal relation." Action, I have tried to show, is inevitably "temporal." Any action is situated or framed within an horizon of *anticipations* and *retentions*. Actions always emerge out of what has just been and are aimed at goals which are not yet. For example, having finished lunch, I paid the bill, picked up my coat and hat, and headed back to the office to finish the report the accounting division was expecting. Thus, a halo of already-having-been-ness or retentions and not-yet-ness or anticipations surrounds and contextualizes our acts. Each act "corefers" to what preceded it and what is about to follow it. "Heading back to the office" is an action or series of actions which refers back to those retained actions sinking back behind it which anticipated it (e.g., paying the bill, and picking up my coat and hat), and ahead to the office and finishing the report which the action itself anticipates or reaches toward. Each present action is pregnant with a "coreferentiality" which links temporality or the temporal relation into a unified series which is "mine."

All of this is lived through on an apperceived or preconscious level. In my everyday actions, I am not conscious *of* them reflectively unless and until I bring them to explicit consciousness through reflective "recall" or "expectation." I do not think about such activity, I *do* it.

Actions, therefore, do not so much exist "in" time as they exist *temporally*. In other words, our actions are a temporal process whereby what has just been the case is transcended in the *action* itself toward what is intended or anticipated by the action. Actions are a sort of temporal relation between what has been and what is not yet.

Insofar as self or subjectivity involves this first "temporal relation," it is constituted in and through *action*. The self is *dynamic*. As Rollo May puts it:

> The 'I can' and 'I will' are the essential experiences of identity. This saves us from the untenable position in therapy of assuming that the patient develops a sense of identity and *then* acts. On the contrary, he experiences the identity *in* the action.[3]

Selfhood: Hegel and Kierkegaard (Los Angeles: University of California Press, 1980); and Mark C. Taylor, *Kierkegaard's Pseudonymous Authorship: A Study of Time and the Self* (Princeton, NJ: Princeton University Press, 1975), esp. pp. 5, 110, 356. Also, see Kierkegaard's *Fear and Trembling and The Sickness Unto Death*, trans. Walter Lowrie (Princeton, NJ: Princeton University Press, 1974), esp. pp. 146ff.

[3] Rollo May, *Love and Will* (New York: W. W. Norton and Company, Inc., 1969), pp. 243–44.

The self is not an empty starting point for actions, but is tied to the temporal relation which in fact structures and shapes those acts. Action and subjectivity are indissolubly linked. The notion of a self-identical subject or soul-substance apart from or before action posited to account for the unity across fragmented and unrelated actions, which "pop up" from moment to moment, is an unnecessary figment of human imagination founded on a wrong-headed conception of time. The self is necessarily tied up with action and thus in part is constituted by the temporality which informs it.

Furthermore, insofar as a self is tied up with this first temporal relation, it is inevitably *tensed.* Actions are temporal. That means that they are never simply fragmentary and momentary, but always "corefer" to what has just been and what is not yet. Actions are temporal *relations* which bridge the past to the future through the present. I cannot emphasize enough that the view that actions and thus selves are locked up in present moments is based upon a picture of time which is false to the phenomenological data.

In fact, since actions *are* temporal and thus beyond merely "present" moments, and since the self involves this primary temporal relation, a self is likewise temporal and tensed. No self is an acosmic and eternal observer outside temporal process for the reason that *the very notion of self involves memory, decision, and anticipation.* There is no existing or personal identity which does not have its own history and anticipated future as part of itself. Remembering my history and anticipating a future I am seeking to appropriate are essential elements of "me." I am who I am because of who I have been in the past and who I shall be in the future. As I said, "I" am a story in the process of happening.

> Whatever else the self is, it is hardly a substance which, in Descartes' phrase, 'requires nothing but itself in order to exist,' nor is it altogether without intrinsic temporal structure. To the contrary, the very being of the self is relational . . . and it is nothing if not a process of change involving the distinct modes of present, past and future.[4]

"The self is a temporal relation." But it is not just that. It is "also a reflective relationship and attitude *to* that," a second relation to the first "temporal" relation. The self is not merely the progressive synthesis of the past and the future in action, *but a relational awareness of and attitude toward itself.* We are not merely preconscious temporal actions, but also what I have called here "a reflective relation" to that.

As I indicated, our immediate, temporal activity is *not* at one and the same time *explicitly* conscious of itself, but is rather apperceived. That means that in acting in the world, I am that action rather than a

---

[4] Schubert M. Ogden, *The Reality of God* (San Francisco: Harper & Row, 1977), p. 57.

conscious reflection upon it; but I can shift my action to a secondary reflective consciousness of that earlier action, thereby making conscious and explicit what was formerly only apperceived and implicit. That means that the manifold of preconscious temporal actions complete with their coreferential horizons of retentions and anticipations, including ultimate life-values which we strive to bring into being, can be consulted and made explicitly conscious by means of a secondary reflective relationship to itself. One special kind of temporal action, then, is the recuperative, conscious, reflective recall of the primary temporal relation.

As an act of consciousness, this reflective recall is "intentional," and thus a *relation* of a conscious "subject" and a known "object." Consciousness of any kind entails consciousness *of* something, a correlative relation of an aware subject (perceiver, recaller, thinker) and an "intended" or "meant" object (something perceived, the past, an idea). As I pointed out, an intentional relation not only relates, but also *separates*; the subject is *not* and can never be the object and *vice versa*.

In the words of Teilhard de Chardin, the reflective relation is a power at the heart of our temporal being,

> a power acquired by consciousness to turn in upon itself, to take possession of itself *as an object* endowed with its own particular consistency and value: no longer merely to know, but to know oneself; no longer merely to know, but to know that one knows.[5]

What is the significance of this reflective power at the center of our lives?

First of all, as I have already indicated, this reflective relation is "recuperative." It makes possible the explicit consciousness of what was until then merely implicit and preconscious. For example, I was running to catch the bus; now that you ask me, I am no longer running, but reflectively recalling that that is what I was doing.

Secondly, we have just seen that as an act of intentional consciousness reflection both relates and separates. Thus, it introduces a sort of negative distance or gulf into the heart of our being and selves; to be a self is not simply to be preconscious, temporal activity, but also to be reflectively conscious *of* that through the secondary act of reflective recall. To be reflectively conscious means that a sort of distance from oneself (as a merely temporal relation) erupts into being, what Sartre has picturesquely referred to as a "hole in being." For example, insofar as I reflectively recall running for the bus, I am related to the "running" intentionally; but at the same time, I am not or no longer that running, but a reflective recollection *of* it.

---

[5] Teilhard de Chardin, *The Phenomenon of Man*, p. 165.

The reflecting relation also permits one "to know oneself," as Teil-hard de Chardin put it, to be *self*-conscious. Now we are getting close to the heart of the matter. What does it mean to be "self-conscious"?

It does not mean to be aware of a kind of static self-identity over time which one can reflectively bump into at this or that moment. Per-ceiving the self in self-consciousness is not like finally perceiving a trunk in a darkened attic by turning on the light. The self, as I said earlier, is not a sort of static object-entity which is always there just waiting for the light of reflection to be perceived. Rather, it is a double set of relations, a reflective relation to its own temporally relational actions.

Hume missed just this point, it seems to me, and erred on two counts. First of all, he was wrong insofar as he pictured time as a linear series of fragmented moments like the ticks of a clock. There is a real *seriality* or *difference* within the flow of our temporal experience, but there is also *unity* or *continuity* through the horizons of coreferentiality which are an implicit part of our temporal actions themselves. Time is *not* a series of independent beads on a string with unbridgeable gulfs between.

Hume was also wrong insofar as he assumed that a self is a sort of static self-identity just waiting to be perceived. Of course, Hume could not perceive or "catch" such an entity-self either in a particular, frag-mented moment; or "over" those moments as a transcendental self. He then became "lost" in a "conceptual labrynth." Part of his problem was that he assumed a wrong-headed notion of "self" and then felt confused and "lost" when he could not find it.

We now have some notion of what self-consciousness does not mean. But we still must ask what it does mean. First of all, to be self-conscious means to be aware of oneself as a temporal relation, or rather, a set of narratively shaped active temporal relations in the progressive tense. John, we might imagine, is that particular person who entered the army in 1941. He was only seventeen and he had to lie to the army as well as his parents to carry it off. He went through bootcamp at Camp Drum and hated it but was determined not to show it; landed in North Africa and fought up through Sicily and Italy; married Gloria when he got home after the war and before going to Princeton on the G. I. Bill; and so on. In part, John is precisely this set of retained, interconnected and yet successive, temporal actions which he can reflectively recall. Indeed, we would call this a small piece of John's autobiography. John is the series of retained temporal actions.

But it is not just the past which makes up the temporal relation which is part of the structure of self. Through the reflective relation, we become conscious of ourselves as also *anticipatory*, as "not-yet" or merely "possible." This too is part of the temporal relation and thus our-selves. Our actions are always anticipating or aimed at goals, including life-values. That anticipation is part of the horizon of "coreferentiality" in any action, is retained as such, and can be brought to consciousness in reflective recall.

To be a self, therefore, means to have a future as well as a past. Karl Jaspers has commented that a person is always more than you can say about him. He or she *is* that because one dimension of him or her is sheer "possibility," "not-yetness," or "existentiality" as Heidegger would put it. To be a self or person includes the sense of *possibility* and *agency*, the sense of what Kierkegaard called "being able,"[6] and that is built right into the temporal relation which structures our everyday activity. To be self-conscious is to be aware of one's past temporal actions, one's anticipated goals, and oneself as in part "possibility" or "openness" itself, the not-yet-finished aspect of a person and real life.

Self-consciousness means reflective awareness of oneself as a temporal relation. But it also means becoming reflectively conscious that we are just such a *double relation* of temporality and reflection. As we have seen, reflection is itself a kind of temporal doing within the stream of our temporal activities and thus itself is retained and reflectively recallable. For example, first I was running for the bus. Then you asked me what I was doing, and I reflectively recalled that I had been running for the bus. Now, I am recalling that whole series, including the earlier act of reflection. In self-consciousness I become aware of myself, not as a thing persisting through time, but as a double relation. *"I" am just this set of temporal activities along with a reflective relationship to it as part of that flow.*

Of course, by means of this self-consciousness of myself as a double relation, I am at the same time aware of the reflective distance or transcendence at the core of myself, because consciousness "separates" as well as relates. In other words, I am aware of a certain stepping back from myself within myself which is both the glory and the burden of my life. The burden is that I can never just *be*, like a tree or a ball of string waiting for *events* to determine or unwind me; there is always a certain *restlessness* in ourselves, a certain gap or distance between what we have been as temporal actions and ourselves as reflective relations *to* that. The glory, as Pascal knew, is that we are aware of all this.

> Man is but a reed, the most feeble thing in nature; but he is a thinking reed. The entire universe need not arm itself to crush him. A vapour, a drop of water suffices to kill him. But if the universe were to crush him, man would still be more noble than that which killed him, because he knows that he dies and the

---

[6] Søren Kierkegaard, *The Concept of Dread*, trans. Walter Lowrie (Princeton, NJ: Princeton University Press, 1957), p. 40.

advantage which the universe has over him; the universe knows
nothing of this.[7]

As we have seen, the secondary reflective relation is *recuperative*,
intrudes a certain *separation* or *transcendence* within the self, and
finally permits the range of *self-consciousness*. We should also emphasize that the reflective relation, by making us aware of the anticipated
future, also brings us face to face with the faith dimension of the self in
which our actions are pervaded by attitudes and life-values. Through
reflection, we can bring to consciousness not just the immediately anticipated ends which our actions "seek," but more ultimate goals and pur-
poses of our actions and lives. These lie within our actions as what they
are "for," as we put it in Chapter Six, the sense of what "counts" or is
fundamentally "good" and "true" and normative for life—a vision of life
and being.

*This means that life-values and attitudes are necessary components
of any self or person.* One can be a self only in faith because selfness
involves the temporal relation, and that in turn is precisely aimed at an
ultimate sense of significance. "To exist as a self is possible only on the
basis of faith."[8] We often learn more about a person's faith by observing
his or her behavior than by listening to his or her words about it, precisely because our actions are shot through with life-value. Our actions
disclose in the doing a basic attitude toward life.

And this is why we argued in Chapter Six that what we called "personal identity" is a kind of story. A person's story has a total meaning
strung through the events themselves which shapes and orders the narrative. Our active, temporal lives are shot through with a meaning or ultimate purpose, a sense of what it is "for" or what we care about which
shapes the actions into a narrative plot. Such an attitude toward life
characterizes "me," constitutes the substance of who "I" am or "personal
identity." Getting to know "me" means getting to know that thematic
vision of life, that fundamental stance in my life which threads my
actions together into a temporal whole, "me."

This narrative meaning or ultimate vision of life and being which
lies sleeping within my very behavior, then, is an attitude which constitutes who I am. When such a life-value changes, "I" change; and that
change shows up in (as it were) a reinterpretation of the remembered
series of personal events, a new life-story. The whole series of past temporal actions gets "seen" differently, becomes part of a different sense of
life or self. The earlier attitude which "had" construed the events far
differently is retained intact, however, but now within a new narrative
meaning or thematic vision of what it is all about. In other words,

---

[7] *Pascal's Pensées*, trans. W. F. Trotter (New York: E. P. Dutton, 1958), p. 97, no. 347.
[8] S. Ogden, *The Reality of God*, p. 114.

although "I" may change by altering my basic attitude, "I" do not thereby forget who "I" used to be, but rather integrate that into the new thematic whole which I forge through my actions.

Insofar as I act toward an ultimate sense of what life and reality is— insofar as my actions embody an attitude toward life, what "I" care about—then I make myself, I become just this personal identity. As Simone Weil put it: "To exist, to think, to know are only aspects of a single reality: to be able to act. . . . From the moment that I act, I make myself exist. . . . What I am is defined by what I can do."[9]

Far from being a thing, the self is in fact a complex set of relations. It is a dynamic process, a set of intentional activities reflectively aware of itself as such. I am a relation which is temporal, but I am also conscious *of* that.

> It is of the essence of time to be not only actual time, or time which flows, but also time which is aware of itself, for the explosion or dehiscence of the present towards a future is the archetype of the *relationship of self to self*, and it shows up an interiority of ipseity.[10]

Finally, as we indicated, over against this necessary, existential, double-relational structure, each of us becomes just this particular personal identity which he or she is. Schubert Ogden brilliantly and briefly catches hold and summarizes the life of such a self.

> I know myself immediately only as an ever-changing sequence of occasions of experience, each of which is the present integration of remembered past and anticipated future into a new whole of significance. My life history continually leads through moments of decision in which I must somehow determine what both I and those to whom I am related are to be. Selecting from the heritage of the already actual and the wealth of possibility awaiting realization, I freely fashion myself in creative interaction with a universe of others who also are not dead but alive.[11]

A Re-Examination of the Issues

We have now seen, at least in outline, something of the nature and structure of subjectivity from the point of view of our phenomenological exploration of time and action. We have only one more task to complete in order to finish our analysis. Earlier, we sketched out four typical and traditional issues with which any adequate philosophical treatment of self must come to grips: *the unity question, the identity issue, the problem of self-deception,* and *the problem of attitude.* What remains for

[9] Simone Weil, *Sur la Science* (Paris: Gallimard, 1966), p. 55. Author's translation.

[10] Merleau-Ponty, *Phenomenology of Perception*, p. 426.

[11] S. Ogden, *The Reality of God*, p. 114.

us, in conclusion, is to indicate how our temporal and relational conception of self is able to deal with these four philosophical problems. Naturally, we can do no more here than point to the kind of resolution our view of self suggests. The more extensive treatment each of these issues deserves must wait for another occasion.

1. The Unity Question

The question is, what unites a present self with his or her different past self? As we put it, "how is it possible . . . that something which over time is very *different* from what it was before is yet the *same*?"

As we (and Bergson) have pointed out, the tradition has tended to divide on this issue into two dialectical extremes. First of all, there are the empiricists such as Locke and Hume who—in part at least because they see time as a linear series of discrete moments—construct the self out of present memories.[12] Thus, unity and continuity *over* time is generated out of fragmented, atomic, different momentary psychic contents.

The second and dialectically opposed extreme is that of such "rationalists" or "idealists" as, for example, Thomas Reid or Kant. Here, over against a background which includes much the same view of time, the unity or self-identity of self *over* time is stressed as opposed to *difference* and seriality within the changing moments. The self, from this point of view, is "pure" and "transcendental," an observer-identity which as such remains above the fray of real difference in time. But these positions are both extravagant and false to our experience. Through the horizon of co-referentiality, our temporal actions include *both* a unity which binds them into this one life (mine) as well as seriality and difference between the actions. Yet those *successive* actions are *successive* only within the framework of a coreferential unity which binds them together as *mine* and as the "before" of this "after" and *vice versa*.

Our position is twofold. First of all, we claim that our phenomenological analysis of temporal action gives us the descriptive means to come to terms with the heart of the issue. We *can* deal with the so-called problem of how a self can be both unity and difference because it just turns out that we *are* that; and the description of it, far from being paradoxical and contradictory, is at least straightforward if not even a little humdrum. But secondly, we are claiming here that the self is neither a sheer, discrete, and momentary psyche which invents a unity for itself like its own shadow nor a pure unity outside of and before such difference. Rather, it is a *"combination" which in fact is the ground for the possibility of either or both positions!* In other words, both views seem

---

[12] For example, see John Locke, "Of Identity and Diversity," *Essay Concerning Human Understanding*, in J. Perry, *Personal Identity*, p. 39.

to be half-truths which are abstracted out of and yet presuppose some-thing like their "combination" within our real, temporal experience. The strength of the empiricists' view, after all, is that it is built upon a truth: there *is* difference over time and thus within any self. Likewise, the strength of the idealists' position is that of course there must be (and *is*) continuity or sameness throughout the life of a self. But these strengths are simply reflections of the temporal experience which we have tried to make reflectively available. Yet, neither of the extremes pays attention to that experience, except to abstract out of it and explain it in terms of a half-truth which presupposes it.

2. The Identity Issue

I know "I" am "I" without comparing myself now to myself earlier. When I awake in the morning, I know I am I before recalling me the night before. The question is, what are the characteristics which make of a person or self just this self-same, particular person or self he or she happens to be at any particular moment?

For a number of reasons I think this is a false issue, at least in the usual way it has come to be phrased. First of all, the very question is shot through with positivistic assumptions and presuppositions. It frag-ments experience into atomic moments (that moment "I" know "I" am "I") and then act *as if* such moments were real. In fact, as we have seen, that is *never* the case.

But secondly, the very phrasing of the question treats the self as a sort of static "thing" with "essential" or defining characteristics which precisely determine it to be what it is. In fact, then, this view *presup-poses* that the self as the observer is a kind of self-identical entity which stands behind the actual psychic changes going on in time. Listen to John Perry's words: "I use identity to mean there is but one thing."[13]

Thirdly, this question assumes that we inevitably *do* "know" that we are ourselves. But that seems farfetched. The psychological literature is full of cases in which a person did not know that "he" was "he," but thought he was the Devil, or Napoleon, or a whole host of different selves or personalities.[14] It seems to me that this question itself presumes what "self" is. This presumption not only leads to the posing of a false issue, but also does not very well account for the evident facts.

Lastly, as we have seen, the self is not a self-identical something or other over or through time. Thus, to the question of what makes a per-son or self just this particular person or self he or she happens to be, we

---

[13] J. Perry, *A Dialogue on Personal Identity and Immortality* (Indianapolis, IN: Hackett Publishing Co., 1978), p. 6.

[14] For example, see Corbett H. Thigpen and Hervey M. Cleckley, *The Three Faces of Eve* (Kingsport, TN: Kingsport Press, 1957).

should answer, "Nothing." In fact, a self, just because it is a double relation, *never* is such an unchanging and static identity over time. On the contrary, because a self is always temporal and inevitably acting toward significant goals or life-values, it necessarily exists narratively, as an emerging and meaningful story "coming from somewhere and going somewhere."

On the other hand, phrased differently, the question is perfectly legitimate and, in fact, resolvable. If what is meant by the question is what makes "Jane" the particular person she is as opposed to "Joyce," for example, then, of course, our temporal and narrative view of self affords us an answer. "Jane" is not a pure identity outside change and experience, *but just this particular autobiography, set of intentions, and fundamental attitude toward life right now in relation to others, her own past and future, and reflectively herself.* "Jane" is not "Joyce" precisely because each of them is a different story. Because each is reaching out toward a different future, each is a different set of narratively construed actions.

3. The Problem of Self-Deception

The problem, you will recall, is what self-deception is and how it is possible. If the two selves (deceiver and deceived) are different, we merely have respectively *lying* (deceiver) and *ignorance* (deceived), but *not self-deception.* On the other hand, if the two selves are one and the same, then that single self seems to be holding contradictory beliefs (both x and -x). As we indicated earlier, we need a conception of self which will permit us to come in between to synthesize both positions: there is a real difference between the deceiving and deceived selves while at the same time there is a unity which binds them together into a single and *self*-deceived subjectivity.[15] I believe that the theory of relational self which we have sketched can help us see just how that is possible.

As a temporal relation, a self is a preconscious set of everyday activities encapsulated within a horizon of retentions and anticipations. Such actions are preconscious, unthematized, merely apperceived, and certainly not a full, reflective consciousness of themselves. On this level, we can be "aware" of what we are doing without being fully conscious *of* it. I can be "angry," for instance, without at the same time being explicitly conscious of the anger.

In fact, such explicit consciousness must await the second relation involved in being a self, the reflective relation. This "self," or aspect of a self, is precisely a making conscious and thematic the as yet merely preconscious and lived. In other words, I can choose reflectively to recall the

---

[15] For more detailed discussion of this, see Alan Paskow, "Towards A Theory of Self-Deception," *Man and World* 12 (1979): 178–91; and Herbert Fingarette, *Self-Deception* (London: Routledge and Kegan Paul, 1969).

anger I felt earlier and become explicitly conscious of it.

In a certain sense our double relational theory of self permits both difference and unity. That temporal aspect of oneself is different from the reflective relational self which can become conscious of it or not. Thus, we can have a preconscious and active side of ourselves which can feel angry while a different, reflective side is not explicitly conscious of that, because it is busy paying selective attention to something else. Thus, our view of self-deception avoids a blatant contradiction precisely because two "different" aspects of self are involved. Furthermore, when I later become conscious of the anger I earlier felt, I can do so because that angry action was a sort of preconscious awareness which I can later reflectively recall in the "aha" experience. The fact that there are two different aspects of self involved, the temporal and the reflective, avoids contradiction and helps us to see how a self could deceive itself and how it could later become aware of that.

On the other hand, there is still a unity here insofar as even the reflective relation is a kind of doing which takes its place within the flow of temporal activity. Through the horizon of coreferential retentions and anticipations that reflective activity is still part of a unity which is strung through those successive actions making them "mine" and "one." Although two different aspects of self are involved in the deception, deceiver and deceived, still this is a *self*-deception. It is not merely "lying" because after all those different aspects of self are only *aspects* of a single, relational whole, "*me*."

4. The Problem of Attitude

The relationship between self and attitude, "personal identity" and one's fundamental life-value or sense of life, should be clear by now. A self determines itself in terms of its fundamental attitude toward life, by what it cares about in its ordinary and everyday behavior. Because it is a double relation, it is never simply a self-identical substance which happens to be whatever it is. Rather, the question of "who" each of us is to become is a radical issue in living, an issue we resolve in our active disclosure of life as ultimately "for" this or that. Stalin's sense of will and domination, we can imagine, is quite different than Thomas Merton's more "mystical" attitude of not willing and letting go. These are different attitudes toward life, attitudes which characterize the behavior of each and which shape that behavior into different stories and different personal identities. As we said in Chapter Two, "of the many remarkable and unique aspects of persons or selves, perhaps the most extraordinary lies in the apparent fact that a self is fundamentally tied up with his or her attitude toward life or life-values."

Acknowledgments

Portions of this book were previously published in different form, as follows:

Chapter 3: "Action and Time," *Man and World*, 10 (1977). Used by permission.

Chapter 5: "The Awareness of Time," *Research in Phenomenology*, vol. XI. Used by permission.

Chapter 6: "Myths and Stories: The Depth Dimension of Our Lives," *Philosophy Today*, 24 (1980), 73–88. Used by permission.